The Haunting of Glamorgan and Gwent

Russell Gascoigne

Gwasg Carreg Gwalch

ISBN: 0-86381-262-7

Cover: Caerphilly Castle

Illustrations by
Commission on Ancient
and Historical Monuments in Wales
and Andrew Gascoigne

First published in 1993 by Gwasg Carreg Gwalch,
Capel Garmon, Llanrwst, Gwynedd, Wales.

☎ (0690) 710261

Printed and published in Wales

Contents

Introduction

This is the second collection of ghost stories which I have compiled. The first, *The Haunting of Sussex*, was a spin-off from a series of locally-based, historical drama-documentaries which I wrote for BBC Radio Sussex while I was living in Brighton. Necessarily, most of the material I came across during the course of my research for the series — although much of it very interesting — I discarded as being unsuitable for dramatisation. One subject, however, continually captured my imagination more than most: ghost stories. Gradually, and almost on a whim, I began collecting them as I went along. Long after I had finished writing my series of drama-documentaries, I continued. And I began, too, to look even further afield in an effort to find out more. I wrote numerous letters, made numerous phone calls and numerous visits to people who offered to assist me. My file on Sussex ghost stories was soon abulge. *The Haunting of Sussex* was the result.

All of this I wrote in my introduction to *The Haunting of Sussex*. As I did much of the following. I repeat it since it holds just as true for *The Haunting of Gwent and Glamorgan*.

As will be apparent by now, I don't make a habit of this. I am not a writer who specialises in writing about the supernatural, the paranormal; it is not a hobby of mine. *The Haunting of Gwent and Glamorgan*, like *The Haunting of Sussex*, I have again written almost on a whim, no more; having moved to Wales, curious to see what stories I could find starting from scratch as it were. Like most people I am not psychic, I have never seen a ghost . . . but I do find them fascinating (another reason for my deciding to return to the subject once more). In writing a book about them, however, there are, of course, pitfalls. To begin with, it is often impossible to give many details about a particular case simply because there aren't any. All that can really be said about the story is that it exists; little more information on the reputed haunting can be revealed other than the fact that it's *there*. It is easy, too, in light of this, to treat what material you do have (after having sorted, as far as possible, the wheat from the chaff, the reliable from the ready-made) simply too sensationally. I hope that in putting this collection together I have at least avoided this latter pitfall if nothing else. I have simply tried to present the facts as I found them. No more. No less.

I say that I have sorted, as far as possible, the wheat from the chaff. And so I have. Even so, those who don't believe in ghosts will argue that this is quite impossible, that all ghost stories fall into the latter category. They have a point. And there are other problems too. Inevitably, ghost stories frequently merge with — are frequently quite indistinguishable from — myths, legends, folk-tales. Often these are patently far-fetched and fanciful, and even the most credulous would be hard pressed to believe there to be any plausibly authentic haunting operating therein. Nevertheless, I have included numerous such stories. Stories in which ghosts appear only in order to reveal the whereabouts of hidden treasure, for instance. My working maxim in this respect has been to regard chaff as consisting not of those stories which stretch the credulity (especially where they have been long established) but, for the most part, those where there is very little evidence of any plausibly authentic haunting, very little tradition of their being any . . . or simply very little story. All highly subjective, certainly, but you have to draw the line somewhere. There has to be some discrimination.

I have made other omissions too. When it comes to certain types of haunting — most of them peculiar to Wales — I have included only a representative selection from among their number. To have included each and every one of them would have entailed endless repetition. There are, for example, the *toili* (a dialect form of the word *teulu* meaning family) — the phantom funeral.

In 1871 (according to Marie Trevelyan who lived in Llantwit Major in South Glamorgan from 1898 until her death in 1922 and who, like her father before her, collected such stories) a woman passing Bethesda church one September evening saw lights in the windows there, a crowd gathered outside in the road. A funeral seemed to be taking place. She had just pressed her way through the crowd when a large white dog suddenly ran out in front of a

7

piebald pony which was standing in the road, causing it to rear up in fright, buck and kick. The entire scene — the crowd, the dog, the pony — then disappeared. In a state of shock the woman ran to nearby Boverton. As soon as she reached a house there, she fainted. Three weeks later a funeral was held at Bethesda church. The woman attended. As the crowd of mourners moved into the road a large white dog suddenly ran out in front of a piebald pony standing there. The pony reared up in fright and began bucking and kicking, scattering gravel everywhere: all just as the woman had seen it three weeks earlier.

In 1836, to give one more example of these stories, the daughter of a Gileston farmer was out walking one night in the area near the Leys. Suddenly she found herself surrounded by deep water. She then saw a group of people accompanying a coffin which they had placed in a boat. They landed the coffin at the backdoor of a farmhouse — and then the vision disappeared. The whole scene had unfolded in absolute silence. (Such visions, if they were seen, weren't usually heard; whereas if a *toili* was heard — through the inexplicable tolling of church bells or the sound of hymns being sung, for example — it usually wasn't seen.) The farmer's daughter knew what it was that she had witnessed. At once she ran home to inform her family of what had happened. Some time later an unusually high tide flooded the Leys and all of the low-lying land between Gileston and Aberthaw. At the same time the body of a person who had died in one of the houses on the Leys was awaiting burial. The road to Gileston church, however, was underwater and was quite impassable. Resourcefully, a group of people duly brought the coffin to the backdoor of the farmhouse in a boat. The farmer's daughter's vision had been re-enacted for real.

These visions are, of course, death omens. It is said that St David prayed that the Welsh should be granted some sign of impending death on occasions so that they could prepare themselves for the unhappy event. Evidently his prayers were answered. There is, in addition to the *toili*, the *cyhiraeth*, a wailing sound which it is said is usually heard by someone closely related to whoever is about to die (or which presages sickness afflicting a neighbourhood, at sea:

8

shipwreck). And there are also the *cannwyll corff* (corpse candles), the appearance of which — ghostly lights flickering in the dark like candles — again, warn of impending death in the household, village or vicinity. For the most part I have omitted all of these. After all, they aren't, strictly speaking, ghost stories to begin with.

But as to what I have included here: little-known stories from the past as well as stories which continue to persist in the present, the patently fanciful (so long as they have a history behind them) as well as the plausibly authentic. Many of these have, of course, appeared in print before. Many more, on the other hand, have not. However, in each case I have tried to draw my information from as close to the original source of the story as possible. And, as I have suggested earlier, I have also tried (within the bounds of compiling what is basically intended to be an entertaining rather than a scholarly collection of ghost stories) to include as much information as possible in each case — although where people have requested that I hold certain details back, I have done.

This isn't, as I have already made clear, an exhaustive collection of Gwent and Glamorgan's ghost stories. It is more a *selection*. And, of course, aside from the stories which I have omitted for whatever reason, there are more still waiting to be discovered. That said, however, the stories collected together here include not only all of Gwent and Glamorgan's best-known stories but also — again, as I have already made clear — many lesser-known ones as well. Many more stories have been included here than have been excluded.

I hope that the result of all this is, as I say, to give an entertaining insight into an engaging subject: the haunting of Gwent and Glamorgan.

Russ Gascoigne
Cardiff

Acknowledgements

My thanks to all of those who either wrote or spoke to me on the subject of any of the ghost stories included in this collection — or who helped in its compilation in any other way. Their contributions were often invaluable. I trust that, collectively, they will accept this acknowledgement of their assistance as a token of my genuine appreciation of their generosity.

Gwent

Some dreams we have are nothing else but dreams,
Unnatural, and full of contradictions;
Yet others of our most romantic schemes
Are something more than fictions.

It might be only on enchanted ground;
It might be merely by a thought's expansion;
But in the spirit, or the flesh, I found
An old deserted Mansion.

No human figure stirr'd, to come or go
No face look'd forth from shut or open casement;
No chimney smoked — there was no sign of Home
From parapet to basement.

With shatter'd panes the grassy court was starr'd;
The time-worn coping-stone had tumbled after;
And thro' the ragged roof the sky shone, barr'd
With naked beam and rafter.

O'er all there hung a shadow and a fear;
A sense of mystery the spirit daunted,
And said, as plain as whisper in the ear,
The place is Haunted!

(From *The Haunted House*, Thomas Hood)

'It was, I think, in the spring of 1894 that my wife and I went
for a bicycling tour along the Wye. In due course, we arrived
at Tintern, where we proposed to stay for a couple of nights.
After luncheon, we inspected the ruins, and paid them a
second visit after dinner, as it was a delicious evening with
brilliant moonlight.'

So begins a story told in *Lord Halifax's Ghost Book* (1937)
concerning the serene and stately ruins of the 12th century
Cistercian abbey at Tintern in the beautiful, densely wooded Wye
valley. The story was privately printed in 1910 originally and was

sent to Lord Halifax, 'apparently by the author', who signed himself merely as E.B.

E.B. went on to reveal that his wife was psychic; at times having the power of automatic writing. This, he wrote, she was reluctant to exercise. The 'beauty and mystery' of the ruins of Tintern Abbey (characterised by majestic arches, towering stone pillars and shaded walkways) compelled him to ask her if she could feel anything there. She could. When they sat down for a moment her right hand was then suddenly seized, as though by an 'invisible agency', and made to rap repeatedly on her knee. She suggested that whoever was controlling her hand be more gentle. E.B., meanwhile, suggested that if anyone was wishing to communicate with them, three taps should be given for the answer 'yes' in response to a question, one for 'no'. At once his wife's hand rose and fell three times — but, obligingly, more gently than before.

This system of communication agreed, E.B. and his wife then asked numerous questions of the spirit which seemed to have contacted the latter and, repeatedly making their way through the alphabet until the spirit tapped her hand on her knee three times, laboriously put its messages together.

From this lengthy question-and-answer session they learned that the spirit was apparently that of a Saxon soldier who had been killed in battle near the abbey while fighting for Henry II. He had been buried, he continued, without prayer or ceremony and asked if a Mass could be said for him. E.B. then asked in return:

' . . . how it was that, after the lapse of many hundred years, he should apply for assistance to a couple of Anglicans whose Church did not include prayers for the dead among its doctrines. He answered that he had frequently, but without success, tried to communicate with his descendants and others, that the difference of religion did not affect the question, and that he would be most grateful if we would have a Mass said for him. This we promised to do; whereupon he thanked us, and bade us good night.'

The following evening E.B. and his wife returned to the ruins.

Once again the latter found her arm being controlled by the Saxon spirit. Once again it expressed its thanks for what the couple were doing for it. It then assured them that if two Masses could be said for it, it wouldn't trouble them again.

A few days later E.B. and his wife returned home to London. A (Catholic) clergyman friend of E.B.'s, Father A . . . , who he had written to from Tintern, met him and informed him that he would say *four* Masses for the spirit of the Saxon soldier.

In time the couple forgot about the spirit, but ten years later they were again reminded of what had happened to them in the Wye valley during the spring of 1895. In November 1905 they held a seance at their home. Two of the ladies who were present were apparently 'possessed of remarkable psychic powers'. One was an intimate friend of the couple, the other they had met for the first time only that evening. E.B. continues:

> 'We sat down. It was not quite dark, for a fire was burning. At first, a number of messages from acquaintances who had passed away were delivered in the usual way by raps or the tilting of the table, until the power seemed to be exhausted and the manifestations ceased. Thereupon, our new acquaintance grew impatient, and pressed with some heat for further messages to be given. My wife protested, pointing out that we should not try to force the power; whatever it might be, it should be treated with courtesy. The table immediately tilted toward her, and slowly rapped out the words 'Very many thanks.' We thought she was being thanked for her remonstrance, but the taps continued. The whole message was 'Very many thanks for the Masses said.' Afterward, the two psychic ladies, who were sitting on either side of my wife, said they had seen standing behind her, the bearded figure of a handsome middle-aged man, dressed in strange close-fitting clothes of gray material. Some years before, we told our story to one of the ladies, but it was not known to anyone else in the room.'

E.B.'s is a colourful story and it serves as an amusing opening to this chapter, certainly. But it can't really be taken too seriously, of course.

On the other hand several people have reported experiences of a rather more traditional sort at the ruins of Tintern Abbey. These stories, perhaps, can't be quite so lightly dismissed.

Over the years various visitors to the ruins have claimed to have seen the grey, hooded figure of a monk there. Custodians at Tintern Abbey — which is now owned by the National Trust — confirm this. The figure is usually said to have been seen kneeling, as though in prayer. Whenever anyone has approached it, it has, apparently, simply vanished from sight.

Turning to the market town of Monmouth to the north, a phantom coach is said to have been seen on a number of occasions on the road leading into the town from the nearby village of Rockfield. In a ghostly re-enactment of a long-ago accident when three passengers aboard a coach were killed after the horses drawing it bolted during a storm, it is said to crash into a wall near Croft-y-Bwlla on dark, stormy nights such as the one when the fateful incident actually took place for real. A second ghostly coach is said to have been seen near Monmouth Forest, on a rough track leading across Upper Bailey Pit.

The Bailey Pits — Old Bailey Pit, Upper Bailey Pit and Lower Bailey Pit — were once the sites of ancient settlements. Old Bailey Pit has now surrendered itself to woodland and all that remains of a medieval farmhouse which once stood on the site are a few low, broken walls. At Upper Bailey Pit, meanwhile, virtually all that remains to mark the site is the only-just-discernible outline of the rough track along which the ghostly coach mentioned in the preceding paragraph is said to travel. It is only at Lower Bailey Pit, then, that a house still stands.

Lower Bailey Pit has the reputation of being the most haunted house in Monmouth; supposedly harbouring at least two separate ghosts. The first is said to be that of a man with a wooden leg who, although never actually seen, has been heard walking noisily around in some of the upstairs rooms. The second is said to be that of a maid who was murdered on the stairs leading down into the cellar. Again, this ghost has never actually been seen, but loud screams are reported to have been heard coming from the cellar — screams so alarming, in fact, that one employee at the farm (as it then was, some years ago) left as soon as he heard the phenomenon.

By the late 1960's the house was deserted, falling into a state of dire disrepair. It was then, according to local amateur historian Stephen Clarke, author of the booklet *The Most Haunted House in Monmouth* (1975) — a Monmouth Archaeological Society publication which gives a detailed account of the alleged haunting of Lower Bailey Pit — that one summer day a plumber cutting off the water supply in one of the outhouses heard a door slam in the house. He went to investigate. He found the house — as he had thought it had been — quite empty. There was no one there. The day being so hot and still it couldn't have been the wind which could have caused the door to slam shut either. There seemed to be no explanation for the event at all. Pushing the door — a door to one of the front downstairs rooms — open again, he prepared to leave. No sooner had he turned his back, however, than the door slammed shut for a second time. This time he didn't even try to investigate the cause; he simply got out of the house as quickly as he could, anxious to spare himself any further such scares. Some time later he returned to the house with both a friend who was interested in the paranormal and Stephen Clarke. Sitting in a downstairs room, it wasn't long before the three heard footsteps, strange tapping sounds and then a loud thud coming from elsewhere in the house. The friend who was interested in the paranormal then said that he sensed a 'presence' in the house — and, warning that it was possibly evil, suggested that they all leave at once. They did so, somewhat to Stephen Clarke's disappointment. Some time later still, however, Stephen Clarke was returning past the house one evening from a nearby archaeological excavation. Once again, he reports, he heard strange sounds coming from inside the house. He peered through the windows on the ground floor, but saw nothing. Telling himself that it was probably only rats which were responsible for the sounds he continued on his way rather than investigate further and actually venture inside the house alone.

In 1970 a local archaeologist told Stephen Clarke about a group of people who, having heard of Lower Bailey Pit's reputation, had visited the house late one night and had ventured inside it; intent on holding a seance there. Stepping into the house out of the drizzle which was falling, the six — three young men, three young women — began their seance in one of the downstairs rooms. Soon, it seems, the atmosphere of the house, or something — began to get to them. It seemed to grow suddenly colder in the room. They claimed to have heard strange noises — some sounding like footsteps — coming from one of the upstairs rooms. They all became more than a little uneasy. And then one of the men, John, became alarmed. 'Let's go,' he said. 'I don't like the feel of this house at all.' With that, all six fled out into the driveway. But once there John's brother, David, turned and shone his torch on one of the upstairs windows. He insisted, quite emphatically, that if there was something in the house, that was where it was. With that, and oblivious to the others' attempts to dissuade him, he ran back into the house. He told one of the group who ran into the hallway after him 'It's my father!' — his voice full of emotion. He then continued hurriedly on up the stairs. By this time John had entered the house too. Suddenly, as he made his way up the stairs, he shouted 'It's coming after me! Shine a torch at it!' On the stairs behind him the wooden treads seemed to strain beneath some invisible weight, the dust there stirred . . . and the sound of heavy footsteps echoed from the walls. He and his companion then ran upstairs as quickly as they could to find David. They found him — in a state of some hysteria — staring into space in one of the bedrooms. All at once a powerful sense of evil seemed to close in on them. They all felt extremely threatened by it. John suggested that they sing. And so they did; singing Bread of Heaven until the 'presence', whatever it was, seemed to fade away. They then left the house and, despite David's repeated attempts to break away from his brother and friends and return to it yet again, they stayed out. Once David had calmed down they made their way home.

nd her wrist. It was by this ring that she was apparent
during 'bouts of madness' (a revelation which rath
r a somewhat different interpretation of her 'character.
known as 'The Lady of the Ring'. After her death h
said to rise from the pool at dusk, dressed in a white dre
appearances presaging a death in the neighbourhoo
terwards.

ls north of Cwmbran there is a deep, reed-filled po
the Pool of Avarice. It is said that many years ago a larg
od nearby. One night, with a storm approaching, a
hed relative of the family living there, knowing that the
aring a lavish meal for some of their friends, knocked
loor. He asked if they would give him some food for h
e was turned away. The storm which had threatened a
hen finally broke. So torrential was the ensuin
that part of Twyn Barllwn, the mountain above th
ped down onto it, burying it completely. There were n
Local tradition has it that on similarly stormy nights th
e dead, punished for their avarice, can still be hear
ound the pool: the spot from which the fateful landslid
descent onto the long-lost house below.
vest of Pontypool is another mountain with a ghost stor
with it: Llanhilleth Mawr. During the 18th century thi
putation of being haunted by one Joan White, anothe
e woman locally regarded as being a witch. It is tha
ould appear on the mountain whenever mist fell over i
d travellers astray there. She was said to wear gre
three-cornered hat and to have an apron thrown bac
oulder.

n Ebbw Vale, a young girl is said to have fallen in lov
n of a wealthy farmer. However, her lover's parent
mined to stifle the realtionship; intent on their so
he daughter of a sea-captain friend of theirs. Even so
ers continued to meet. The farmer's son continued t

David maintained, however, that it was his father who had been in the house — even though his father had died when he was only a baby and he had never known him.

A prank? Play-acting? Or a genuine brush with the paranormal?

Whatever, in the summer of 1973 Lower Bailey Pit was destroyed by fire. Rebuilt, no unusual occurrences have been reported there since.

Remaining in Monmouth, the Queen's Hotel in the town is said to be haunted by the ghost of a would-be assassin of Oliver Cromwell who attempted to murder the Protector when he stayed there one night. The man's shadowy figure has reportedly been seen in the bedroom where the incident took place while, rather more tangibly, bullet holes can still be seen in some of the room's rafters.

Still in the Monmouth area, the banks of the River Wye are said to be haunted both at Dixton on the northern outskirts of Monmouth itself, and at the village of Redbrook which lies just to the south of the town. At Dixton the ghost of a parcel carrying tramp is said to wander the banks of the river near where he drowned many years ago, while at Redbrook, according to local legend, the sounds of a woman's screams have been heard near Swan Pool and, occasionally, the ghosts of a mother and child seen.

Coincidentally, both settlements have other ghosts too, it seems. At Dixton the ghost of a man accompanied by a small dog is reported to have been seen near the church, while at Redbrook a phantom coach (a common phenomenon in the Wye valley, apparently) is said to pass through the village with a beautiful young woman peering through its windows.

At the impressive 14th-16th century mansion that is Llanfihangel Court, north of Abergavenny, there is said to be both the ghost of a White Lady and the ghost of a small green man with green eyes. The latter is said to appear, somewhat inappropriately, in the White Room. The White Lady, meanwhile, is said to appear in the hallway on the stroke of midnight on those occasions when she walks. From there she is said to make her way out onto the terrace, pause for a moment, and then continue along the avenue of Scots firs which leads from the house, until she reaches a small wood adjoining it. There, she disappears. Some accounts of this particular story have it that as she walks out onto the terrace the White Lady not only pauses, but gives a loud scream.

Unlike the Green Man, there is a possible explanation for the appearances — or for the stories — of the White Lady. Many years ago when the terrace across which she walks was undergoing alterations, a skeleton was unearthed there. To add further drama to the discovery, it had a bullet lodged in it. Is this why the White Lady of Llanfihangel Court is said to scream when she steps out onto the terrace? Was she a murder victim, shot dead there? No one knows.

In *Journeys in Gwent* (1951), Fred Hando, who wrote about south-east Wales a great deal in the 1940's and 50's, described a visit which he made to the house (which is, incidentally, still open to the public at certain times of the year). He asked a guide who was showing him around the house if he had seen the White Lady. The guide told him that he hadn't, but that on one occasion his father and the chauffeur had seen a door leading into the hallway open one summer night, seemingly of its own accord, there being no wind or draught which could possibly have accounted for it. The door then closed again. Immediately afterwards the front door then opened and closed in exactly the same manner. Some time later, he concluded — on a similarly still night — his father heard a prolonged scream while he was alone in the house, 'but saw nothing on that occasion'.

The Skirrid Inn in Llanfihangel Crucorney, named after the nearby mountain (Skirrid-fawr) which overlooks it, is often referred to as being the oldest inn in Wales. It is probably more accurate, however, to say only that it is probably one of the earliest sites of an inn in Wales. Writing in *Out and About in Monmouthshire* (1958), for example, Fred Hando said that he couldn't date the present day building much before 1640 or so. Whatever the truth, there was an inn here — if not the present day inn — as early as

1107. It was, apparently, frequented [...] as an informal meeting place. [...] meanwhile, has certainly been the s[...] gatherings. After the Monmouth Re[...] Judge Jeffreys held court here and se[...] out at the inn; those sentenced to dea[...] over the stair well.

One of Judge Jeffreys' victims [...] sentence could be carried out and die[...] inn. The ghost of this — one eyed —[...] Skirrid Inn. But there are other ghos[...] building too. 'Evil forces' are said t[...] years and it used to be the landlord's[...] over the fireplace every night in an[...] other-worldly spirits at bay — a vari[...] upheld in many of the older houses in[...] jug of milk for the local 'Pwcca' (a s[...] every evening. In *Welsh Tales of t[...]* Powell, records that one such 'p[...] knocking at the door of a Monmou[...] winter months. Whenever the farme[...] he would find that was nothing t[...] another farmer — who was a go[...] 'pwcca'. One night when there wer[...] door, it was he who answered. No [...] 'pwcca' threw a rock at him. He wa[...] time the family who lived at the fa[...] their 'pwcca'. As well as knockin[...] began to make music — somethi[...] more readily.

Finally, there is also — or was or[...] and ancient village of Llanfihang[...] concerns a White Lady. In this cas[...] Eleanor. She is thought to have d[...] the 15th century and to have been[...] family. Regarded as being a witch[...]

call on the girl at the house where she lived with her parents. They continued to spend a lot of their time together down by the local mill-stream. The farmer's son — perhaps to placate her, but more probably in order to secure her 'favour' — then played a cruel hoax on the girl. Making her swear to secrecy about the event so that his parents wouldn't find out about it, he married her. The marriage was, however, a false one; he had simply arranged for a friend to conduct a bogus service for the two of them. The girl must have been extremely gullible, certainly — but she believed it all, fell for it without question. Her parents, meanwhile, still believing him — correctly, of course — to have no intention of marrying their daughter, began to regard the son's continued visits to their home with increasing hostility. But, gradually, the son's feelings towards their daughter began to change too. He began to grow indifferent to her. He began to call on her with less and less frequency. Finally, he stopped coming to see her altogether. And he did so before she could inform him of one very important fact: she was pregnant by him.

The child was duly born. The girl's father then threatened to throw her out of the house for the shame which he deemed she had brought to the family. And it was then that the girl broke her promise to the farmer's son not to tell anyone about their secret wedding. At once her father paid the son's father a visit. A heated argument soon led to the wealthy farmer's son having to confess all. The girl's father insisted that the son stand by his daughter. The wealthy farmer, however, insisted that he would still marry the sea-captain's daughter — despite everything. The girl's father left in a fury, dragging his distraught daughter after him.

Shortly before the son's wedding, the girl again met her errant lover, hoping to persuade him to return to her by taking along their baby, which he had never seen. They met, as they had done on so many other occasions, by the mill-stream.

The following day the bodies of both the girl and the baby were found in the stream, drowned. Whether the girl decided to commit suicide because her former lover refused her and decided to take her baby with her, or whether they were both drowned by the farmer's son, isn't known. In any event it seems that the farmer's son went ahead and married the sea-captain's daughter, just as his parents had always intended. But the marriage didn't last beyond the honeymoon. The farmer's son was drowned. And a final ironic twist to the story: it seems that his wife, like the girl who drowned in the mill-stream at Ebbw Vale, was left alone with his baby.

As to the ghostly element of the story: the ghost of the drowned girl is said to have been seen walking along the banks of the mill-stream on several occasions, her baby held in her arms. Described as a 'misty white shape', she is said to walk beneath the bridge which crosses the stream, to then disappear into the nearby churchyard.

In 1958 the Cross Keys Inn at Usk gained some media attention after the then landlord, Roland Hoffmann, reported that one of the rooms there was haunted. The latch on the door of Room 3 would repeatedly lift of its own accord, he claimed, and the door would then open and close.

In November a television camera-crew sat up all night in the room in the hope of recording anything which took place. Early in the morning the candle — which was all the light they had in the room — was blown out, seemingly without cause. They re-lit it. Ten minutes later the same thing happened again. But that was all that did take place.

It was later reavealed that the inn had once been an 11th century hospice attached to Usk Priory. It was further revealed that in the 17th century a priest had been martyred nearby by being hanged, drawn and quartered. It was suggested that it was with this latter event that the haunting of Room 3 was associated. Since then, however, other landlords at the Cross Keys have suggested that the ghost could, in fact, be that of a 16 year-old girl who committed suicide there at some point in the inn's history.

So far as is known, the ghost — whoever, whatever it is — has never actually been seen.

At Chepstow is the St Pierre Golf and Country Club. Here, a Grey Lady, a member of the Lewis family, is said to appear from time to time — usually in a room known as 'The Sturges' (all of the room names in the house are taken from an ancient tithe map).

In keeping with the calm atmosphere which pervades St Pierre, the Grey Lady is regarded as being a wholly benevolent ghost. The earliest known sighting of her was at the end of the 19th century when a lady guest of the Lewis family came down late for breakfast one morning. She saw what she described as 'a little old lady in grey' walking along a passage ahead of her. She assumed that it was the housekeeper, but later learned that no one — not even the housekeeper — had been in that particular part of the house at the time. She had been alone there. What she had seen was the Grey Lady.

In the 1950's, Fred Hando — again — writing a series on Gwent's major houses, is said to have stayed at St Pierre and to have felt a 'presence' there. On two separate occasions, it seems, he slept in a small room at the top of the house and awoke feeling both cold and quite convinced that there was someone in the room who wanted to get out of it.

Maes Fawr (Big Field), a room on the upper floor, is said to have been the scene of a long-ago duel between two more guests at St Pierre, and the room is now reported to be troubled by recurrent poltergeist activity. Tump Ground, another of the rooms in the house, is also said to be haunted. Apparently strange noises have often been heard coming from both of these rooms.

But the stories concering St Pierre's ghosts don't end there. There is also a story of a 'laughing gardener'. The ghostly figure of someone taken to have been a former gardener at the house is said to walk through the gateway leading from the walled garden, cross the road and then disappear into the churchyard there. All the while he is said to be laughing.

During the days of the Roman Empire two legions were stationed in Wales: one at Chester, the other at Caerleon-on-Usk. It was the Second Augustan Legion which was stationed at Caerleon; some

5,500 troops being based at a 50-acre fortress which was established here in about A.D. 75. The sound of the soldiers' footsteps are still said to be heard on occasions at the site of the amphitheatre — the remains of which, like the remains of the fortress and baths, can still be visited.

Newport Castle is said to be haunted by its Norman founder, Robert Fitzhamon. Unaccountably, he is said to appear as a giant — a figure which then vanishes as soon as anyone looks at him.

St Woolos church which overlooks the river Usk on whose banks Newport Castle stands is said to have been built by a famous drunk who lived in the town in the 5th century. One night, local legend has it, he was awoken from a drunken stupor by a voice which instructed him to forsake his evil ways and turn to God. His wife, a religious woman who had prayed for such a turnaround in his character, was overjoyed. And her husband wasn't at all half-hearted about his conversion either. He gave to the poor with such generosity that he became known as St Gwynlliw. He then declared his intention to build a church at the top of Stow Hill overlooking Newport. (Tradition maintains that the site was suggested to St Gwynlliw by an angel as he slept one night. The angel suggested that he should build the church wherever he found a particular ox grazing: a white ox with a single black mark on its forehead.) Once the church was completed he decreed that anyone who stole from it or who desecrated it in any other way would be cursed. The following year he died. Shortly afterwards some pirates sailed up the River Usk. They landed, set about pillaging all that they could from the town. And among the buildings which they ransacked was, of course, St Woolos'. Finally, they set sail again. Once they reached the Bristol Channel, however, they fell foul of the St Gwynlliw's curse. A violent storm blew up and as their ship began to founder under its onslaught the ghost of St Gwynlliw appeared, snatched the various treasures stolen from St Woolos' from its pitching deck and vanished into the clouds. The ship then sank. All of the pirates lost their lives; their bodies being washed up on the banks of the Usk over the course of the next few days. Jane Pugh, who records this story in *Welsh Ghostly Encounters* adds that St Woolos' only suffered one more act of sacrilege after the pirates' raid. During the Civil War one of Cromwell's troops shot the head off a statue which stood in a niche in the church tower. The head is still missing.

Just outside Newport is the village of Whitsun. Here the ghost of one Eva Roberts was once said to haunt the house which is now the village post office. Apparently an exorcism was carried out at the house and Eva appeared. Villagers then chased her across the moors north of the village. They had, the story continues, almost caught up with her when she dived into a well which then stood at the end of Batchelor Road on the outskirts of Newport. She was never seen again. From then on the well became known as Ffynnon Eva. In time it gave its name to the whole of the surrounding area: Eveswell.

Glamorgan

I pray you now all, great people and small,
Give ear to my narration,
A spectral thing is what I shall sing,
The wonder of all the nation;
And such a rum Ghost is its pride and boast,
Is beating the boards and the benches;
Both Old Men and Boys have heard the noise,
And so have a good many wenches.

Chorus, Tiddly tol lol

In Llanblethian House with D — n and his spouse
The ghost is now residing,
He has left his tomb for a nice bed room;
And there is at present hiding,
All day he's quiet and makes no riot,
Like a decent ghost behaving,
But at then o'clock he begins to knock
With scratching and thumping and shaving.

Chorus, Tiddly tol lol
(Llanblethian Ghost — A New Song, Anon)

South Glamorgan

A Roman fort once stood on the site where Cardiff Castle now stands. Part of the castle — the keep, to be precise — is of Norman origin. The rest of the castle, however, is really no more than an elaborate folly, built during the Victorian era.

Having made his fortune (and Cardiff's) by exporting coal all over the world from the city's docks — the area around which now bears his name: Butetown — the second Marquess of Bute instructed that the ruins of the Norman castle be completely restored, but not to their original state; in the romanticised manner of the Middle Ages.

He never saw his dream realised. In 1848 he collapsed and died in his dressing-room at the castle, leaving it to his son to continue and complete the project. In 1861, then, the third Marquess of Bute engaged the architect William Burgess to fashion the castle into the impressive palace that it is today, standing in the very centre of the city of Cardiff, its crowning Victorian monument. The Bute family left the castle in 1947 and it is now cared for by the City of Cardiff. With its spectacular assemblage of different architectural styles, its lavishly decorated interiors and peacocks strutting and calling in its grounds, it has become a major tourist attraction.

The most well-known ghost story connected with the castle concerns the second Marquess of Bute. His ghost is said to appear through the fireplace in the Library, pass through a six foot thick wall, cross a corridor and then make its way through yet another wall to enter the room where he died — converted, after his death and in his memory, into a private chapel by his son.

There is also a Grey Lady reputed to haunt the castle. Variously described as being a 'nun-like' figure, a 'faceless vision in flowing greyish-white skirts', or simply as a 'lady in grey', it is she who is thought to be responsible for numerous disturbances which have been reported in the main dining-hall and its adjoining ante-room. In the early hours of the morning heavy doors have apparently opened and closed by themselves and lights have been repeatedly switched on and off. In addition footsteps and other strange sounds have been heard there too. In January 1973 the *Cardiff Leader* reported that former custodian Derek Edwards had an alsatian which he used to take with him on his rounds late at night. The dog, it seems, would often refuse to enter either the Banqueting Hall or the Library. His predecessor, Edgar Donne, said Mr Edwards, had had similar problems; his dog wouldn't enter the Library at night either and would snarl and bristle outside the door. Mr Edwards added that although he had never actually seen the ghost he had on one occasion seen a grey 'form' standing at the foot of his bed — which then vanished as soon as he looked at it.

In 1984 the custodians at the castle were Gordon and Beryl Gray. In September 1984 the *South Wales Echo* reported that they too had had some strange experiences there. Beryl Gray said that, on two separate occasions, she had seen a grey nun-like figure in the ladies toilets. In a stock-room near the Banqueting Hall, she went on, various items would frequently be rearranged by some 'presence' there. She decided that the ghost was that of a maid and christened her 'Sarah'. On one occasion she felt Sarah tapping her on the shoulder while she was in the stock-room. On another occasion she saw her in a mirror. Turning, she found that there was no one there. When she looked back in the mirror, the figure she had seen was there again — but had moved closer to her. On both occasions, she concluded, she had told Sarah to 'go away'. Sarah had duly obliged.

A second Grey Lady is said to appear outside the castle walls: on the bridge over the River Taff. There, after having walked through Queen Street and then along Duke Street (at both of which locations she is also supposed to have been seen), she is said to pause and wave towards the castle before disappearing. It has been suggested that she could be the ghost of Elizabeth de Burgh, one of three sisters of Gilbert de Clare (III) who held the castle in the early 12th century. It has also been suggested, on the other hand, that she is the ghost of someone who was close — either by relation or affection — to Robert, Duke of Normandy, the eldest son of

William the Conqueror. After being imprisoned at various locations around England for opposing his brother Henry I's succession to the throne, he was brought to Cardiff Castle in 1126, where he then remained until his death in 1134. According to some sources he was well treated during his imprisonment at the castle. Other sources have it that he was treated rather less well; even having his eyes put out 'by order of his cruel brother, Henry'.

Finally, to round off this roll-call of ghost stories at Cardiff Castle, a phantom coach is said to cross the bridge over the Taff and then enter the castle forecourt whenever a member of the Bute family is about to die (and, interestingly, a similar phenomenon is said to occur at the family's home, Dumfries House, in Ayrshire, Scotland, too). In May 1956 the *Empire News* carried a story that a David Brecon had reported seeing a coach and four on the bridge one winter night. On the 10th November 1868, he later learned, a trustee at the castle, a Mr Boyle, heard the coach arriving at the castle while he was in the Library. He asked the butler who it was — only to be told that no coach had arrived, that the forecourt was empty. Mr Boyle insisted, however, that he had heard the clatter of horses hooves, the rattle of harnesses . . . even the sound of the coachman's horn. That evening Lady Sophia, daughter of the first Marquess of Hastings, second wife of the second Marquess of Bute and the mother of the third Marquess of Bute, died. In 1900, the article concluded, Lady Margaret, the only daughter of the third Marquess of Bute, heard the phantom coach on the eve of her father's death at Dumfries House.

The current Administrator at Cardiff Castle reports that 'we have no record of any strange occurrences of any nature at the Castle in recent years'.

Barely more than a stone's throw from the castle the National Museum of Wales, opened in 1922, stands shoulder to shoulder with Cardiff's ornate City Hall between the peaceful Cathays Park and the busy Boulevard de Nantes. Here too there is said to be a ghost — in this instance, of rather more recent provenance. The ghost is thought to be that of the architect who designed the building, Dunbar Smith. Taking umbrage at his ashes — originally interred in a casket in the central block — being moved

29

to a new position near the gents toilets, his ghost is thought to be responsible for a number of strange occurrences which have taken place in the building: lifts setting off of their own accord, telephones ringing and then stopping again, a television in the archaeological department turning itself on after the cleaners had left. In addition, warders have complained of a chair repeatedly being moved from beneath a desk in the zoology department during the night and left in the middle of the floor, perfume has been smelled in an ante-room and strange tapping sounds have been heard on the roof in the early hours of the morning (seagulls, suggested one warder). To top it all, one of the warders has actually reported seeing the ghost. Checking that there were no visitors left in the archaeology department one evening when the museum was about to close for the day, he walked through the gallery and found it quite deserted. But then something made him turn and look back. He saw what he described as a 'tall, thin man in black' standing in front of one of the display cases. The figure then disappeared. At once the warder went to investigate. He found that the gallery was deserted. No one had been there.

Llandaff, north west of the city centre was once a small village. The village green can still be seen there and so, too, can many of the village's ancient buildings. Cardiff Cathedral can be found here along with the ruins of an old priory. And so can a number of ghost stories. No less than three of these concern drownings in the River Taff. The first ghost is said to be that of a grief-stricken woman whose only son drowned in the river and whose body was never recovered from it. She is said to haunt both the cathedral grounds near Choristers Hall and the banks of the river itself near the weir — where she repeatedly paces up and down as though in search of her lost son's body. The second is 'Bella', thought to have been the wife of a landlord of a long-demolished pub in Llandaff who, finding religion, turned against drinking, gambling and all of the other vices to be found in her husband's hostelry, argued with him over it one evening and then ran out and drowned herself in the river. Her ghost is now said to haunt the riverbank too. Finally, there is the curiously named 'Frog Lady of Llandaff'. In life this unfortunate woman — who, it seems, came from a well-respected family in the village — was both mentally and physically handicapped. She was so named, it is said, because she moved around in a series of frog-like leaps, croaking while doing so. Cruelly put out for adoption in the home of a local agricultural labourer by her family, she fell into the river one night — and she too was drowned. Her ghost is now reputed to haunt the riverbanks on moonlit nights, both above and below the weir.

Two other ghost stories in Llandaff both concern pubs which can still be found there. That said, however, perhaps the first — a story connected with the Cow and Snuffers — shouldn't be classified as being a ghost story at all. The subject of ancient Welsh death omens was aired in the introduction — the *Gwrach y Rhibyn* (*Gwrach* — Witch, *Rhibyn* — Curse) is another such omen. A hideous, leathern-winged hag with matted hair, glaring eyes and spindly arms, this terrifying creature — similar to the Irish banshee — was said only to appear to those of pure Welsh pedigree. Knocking at doors and clawing at windows, the *Gwrach y Rhibyn* would then warn of whoever was about to die by shrieking out their name. It was just such a creature which is said to have visited the Cow and Snuffers (then known by a different name) in 1877. 'A horrible old woman with long red hair and a face like chalk and great teeth like tuskes', she is said to have entered the inn, then owned by the Llewelyn family, through an open window late one night — to then fly wildly around the room letting out ear-splitting shrieks before leaving again through the window. The following night, at exactly the same time, a member of the Llewelyn family died at the inn.

The second story connected with a Llandaff pub concerns the Maltsters Arms. Here the story is of a rather more traditional nature. Originally a malt house, the Maltsters is said to have the ghost of a small, dark man wandering the bars at night. In 1965 the then landlord, Ken Perrett, reported that he had actually seen the figure.

On Cathedral Road in Cardiff's Pontcanna district stands what would seem to be — if all of the stories told about it are true, and Cardiff Castle aside — the most haunted building in the capital.

The former offices of the Automobile Association here are reputed to harbour the ghosts of at least two separate women, a phantom white cat and a resident poltergeist. The first of the two ghostly women was christened 'Alice' by the staff. A young woman, her hair tied back in a bun, wearing a shabby dress and with old-fashioned earphones on her head, she was said to appear in the building quite often, to smile as soon as she was seen — and then vanish. Her appearances were always said to be preceded by a strange, evil smell. Some of those who claimed to have seen Alice reported that she too was evil; her smile, as one person described it, 'perfectly horrible, showing all her teeth'. Others, however, have simply reported that she smiles 'sweetly' before fading away from sight. The second ghostly woman is said to be a nun dressed in a white habit (the building was once part of a convent) who appears most often on the top floor. The phantom white cat, meanwhile, was said to haunt a flat adjoining the offices; running unhindered through the walls there. It was the flat, too, which was once affected by a flurry of poltergeist activity. The wife of one of the road managers reported that furniture and ornaments were repeatedly being moved around the flat and doors slammed shut. On one occasion, she complained, chairs were actually thrown through the air. Even more dramatically perhaps, she said that when she went to switch on the heater one night, a ghostly hand appeared next to her own. Her husband being out on duty, she ran into the main office vowing never to return to the flat again.

All of these events were reported in the *South Wales Echo* — in October 1965, again in 1986. Officially, the AA has always dismissed talk of the building being haunted. Many people who worked there, however, confirm having heard loud noises coming from empty rooms on the upper floor of the building while working there late at night, having found chairs — which had been carefully, and securely, stacked against the wall — scattered across a room there and sensing a 'presence' in the building. They are in no doubt that the building is haunted. If it is, presumably further reports of strange occurrences there will soon make themselves known. At the moment, however, it seems that nothing unusual has been either seen or heard there.

Returning towards the city centre once more, the New Theatre is reputed to be haunted by the ghost of an elderly lady. She has apparently been seen on several occasions over the years. Appearing, first of all, in one of the boxes, she is said to behave as though she is looking for something there before walking down the stairs to the stalls where she then disappears again. It is thought that she is the ghost of a woman who fell from — or was found dead in — the box many years ago at the end of a matinee performance at the theatre.

Bob Bunkell, the Stage Manager at the New Theatre reports that some time ago an electrician focusing a spotlight on top of the circle was about to fall when he felt someone grab hold of his legs. Turning to thank whoever it was who had saved him from what could easily have been a very nasty accident, he found that there was no one there. Bob Bunkell adds that he too has had strange experiences at the theatre in the past. On one occasion he saw a door open, seemingly of its own accord, in the circle area. On another occasion, while working at the back of the auditorium, he suddenly felt cold — despite the fact that the theatre was actually quite hot — and sensed a 'presence' nearby. He also reports, however, that since a major renovation of the theatre was completed in 1988 there has been no repetition of any such occurrences. Nor has the ghost of the old lady been seen at all.

Many years ago a Lady in Black was said to haunt one of the old sea locks in the docks. Often seen at dusk, she was said to pace up and down the side of the lock wringing her hands, as though in anguish. One evening, so the story goes, a ship's captain stopped and asked her if there was anything that he could do for her. She told him that if he would take her by boat to the mouth of the River Ely, he would be richly rewarded. The captain duly obliged and rowed her across to a small wood there. The woman then led him into the wood and told him to pick up a large stone which she pointed out to him. He did so. Beneath the stone he found a hoard of gold coins. The Lady in Black then disappeared — never to be seen again.

A second story linked to the Ely has it that the ghost of a boatman who drowned in the river once haunted the moors between Canton and Leckwith. Locals avoided the area if they could, fled in terror whenever they saw the ghost. One night, however, a man not only approached the ghost when he saw it, but actually spoke to it. The ghost told him that his head had been lost, that devils had taken possession of it and were using it as a football on the riverbank each night. Until it was recvered from them, it continued, it couldn't rest in peace. The man promised to help, and that same evening — praying as he approached — interrupted the devils' nightly game. At once the devils fled, leaving the boatman's skull behind them. The man then buried the skull deep in the mud of the riverbank and said a few prayers over it for the dead boatman. The boatman's ghost, like the Lady in Black, was never seen again.

During the Civil War it is said that the Ely ran red with blood after a Royalist army of some 8000 men under the command of Major-General Laugharne were routed by Colonel Horton's Roundheads at the Battle of St Fagans. The sounds of that battle are said to linger at St Fagans still.

It is at St Fagans too that the Welsh Folk Museum (part of the National Museum of Wales) is situated. It is thought by some of the staff there that the site is haunted by the ghost of the first curator of the museum, Dr Peate. The ghost hasn't, it seems, ever been seen clearly, but a 'dark figure' has apparently been seen both at the castle which stands just inside the entrance to the site and at one of the re-erected houses there. A former cleaner at the museum reports that on entering the latter on one occasion she saw the figure — a 'shadowy dark shape' — jump out of an open window. On another occasion, she says, when she was trying to open the same window, something — or someone — seemed to be pushing against it from the other side to keep it shut.

Further south, overlooking Cardiff across the River Ely mudflats and the rapidly developing Cardiff Bay, stands Baron's Court pub-restaurant. Built in the 16th century and originally known as Cogan Pill House, it is said to be haunted by the ghost of a woman who committed suicide by throwing herself from a doorway above what was once the banqueting hall. At Splott, also in the southern part of the city, the ghost of a priest wearing a black cloak and a large black hat is said to haunt Sanquahar Street. At St Mellons, to the east of the city, meanwhile, the ghost of a man was once said to haunt the churchyard there, where he would be seen sitting on the stump of the old stone cross.

Roath Park is said to have had two ghosts haunting it in the past. One was that of a tall woman who would stand beneath the 'ghost tree' at the edge of the lake at midnight when the tree was in full bloom and wave towards the lake with a handkerchief. Tradition has it that her lover drowned while swimming there. The second — another female phantom — has become known as the Grey Lady of Llanishen. It was by holy well of Ffynnon Denis (the waters of which were generally supposed to be extremely efficacious for the treatment of sore eyes and rheumatism) that she was usually said to appear.

In the early 19th century Penylan Well (at Tygwyn Farm) was said to be haunted by a Lady in Black who could frequently be seen there wailing and moaning. Eventually a man stopped and spoke to her. She told him that if he held her by the waist and remained silent whatever happened, she would be released from bondage (it being thought that the firm hand-clasp of a 'pure-minded' man could do this for the spirits of the departed — as could the kiss of a new-born baby). The man did as he was asked and put his arm around the woman's waist. Almost at once, however, he felt a sharp, stabbing pain in his arm and was forced to let go of her. The Lady in Black fled in horror, screaming that it would take her another two hundred years before she could again be freed.

In woods alongside the Melingriffith-Tongwynlais footpath there was once a spring known as the White Lady's Well. It was, of course, named after a ghostly White Lady who was said to haunt it. The ghost was thought to have been that of a woman who was stabbed to death nearby by her lover. Tradition had it that a stone placed in the water of the spring would turn red because of her blood. And so it would — but only, of course, because of iron oxide in the water. A second 'Ladi Wen' (White Lady) was said to haunt Radr Ford, a third the Tithe Barn which once stood near the entrance to the present day Whitchurch Hospital.

It was at the Tithe Barn too that a farm labourer by the name of Draper apparently hanged himself from a rafter in the early 19th century. According to tradition, his ghost then haunted both the barn and the road leading from there on to Tongwynlais. In around 1866 it seems that there was considerable consternation in the area after the ghost was said to have been seen on several occasions both on the road and in surrounding woods and fields. Eventually a ghost hunt was organised. The 'ghost' was caught. It turned out to be an impoverished mad woman who lived in the neighbourhood and whose wont it was to wander about the area at night, even in the most inclement weather.

That said, a member of the Lewis family who used to live at Greenmeadow in Tongwynlais (about which more in a moment) was convinced that there was a ghost haunting the barn. She described how Greenmeadow horses drawing carriages past the barn would often take fright there and then gallop out of control past their home gates as well, only coming to a halt again when they reached 'the shop in Tongwynlais owned by old Mrs Bond', by which time they would be covered in sweat.

Which brings us to Tongwynlais itself.

Noted primarily for its picturesque castle, Castell Coch (again, about which more in a moment), Tongwynlais can also lay claim to possibly having had one of the most haunted houses in South Wales standing on its outskirts: Greenmeadow.

Originally a 17th century farmhouse known as Pantgwynlais, Greenmeadow (nicknamed Pantgwynlais Castle by locals) was an imposing, romantic mansion set in its own sumptuous grounds on the southern edge of the village. It was the home of the Lewis family for over a century. In the early 19th century it was owned by Wyndham Lewis who became the M.P. for the Glamorgan Boroughs in 1820. It was in the same year too that an imposing facade was added to the original building and the house renamed Greenmeadow by his wife, Mary Anne Lewis — all to celebrate the event. After his death in 1838, Greenmeadow then achieved some notable national notoriety when his former political colleague

Benjamin Disraeli began openly conducting a relationship with his young widow. It was widely suspected that the two had been having an affair long before Wyndham Lewis' death. Less than a year later they were married. Greenmeadow was then inherited by Wyndham Lewis' brother, Henry.

In 1860 the Melingriffith Band played at an annual supper held at Greenmeadow by Henry Lewis. Being so engaged by a member of the gentry was an enormous fillip to the band and, accordingly, they presented themselves at the house dressed in their best clothes and having equipped themselves with brand new instruments for the occasion.

The supper was an unqualified success. Afterwards — and no doubt in high spirits — the members of the band made their way homeward along the tree-lined driveway which led from the house. Suddenly, however, they were confronted by a shimmering apparition which they later described as being 'fierce, foul and awful'. They dropped their instruments such was their panic to escape and fled in terror — only daring to return to retrieve their instruments the following day. Many refused to venture along the driveway at night ever again.

A second curious incident told about the house concerns one Daniel, an old gardener who had been employed by the Lewis family for all of his working life. One morning he was found dead in the grounds — in part of the garden which, for some reason, he had always refused any of the children of the house to go near and which he regarded with little disguised fear. When he was found he is said to have had a look of absolute terror on his face. He had, said the coroner, died of heart failure. And so he might have done. The fact that some of Greenmeadow's dogs were found lying dead alongside him, however, added a somewhat sinister twist to the matter. Had he — had they — seen whatever it was that had scared off the Melingriffith Band on Greenmeadow Drive?

In 1886 a Captain Mostyn, a 'brave hero of Rorke's Drift', stayed at Greenmeadow, in the Oak Room. In the early hours of dawn it is said that he was awoken by three heavy thuds on the door. He looked up and saw a tall red-haired man leaning on a sword by the window, looking out into the garden. Suddenly the figure dropped his sword and, crossing himself, fell to his knees as if in prayer. He then disappeared.

Over breakfast that morning, the story continues, Henry Lewis informed his guest that the figure was a common apparition at Greenmeadow — but asked him not to mention his experience of it as it would upset the servants. He then added that the house was haunted by other ghosts too — including both a hunch-backed figure who appeared in the cellar and the ghost of a former servant (dressed in the household's green livery) who would appear in the Blue Room.

Further back still in time, in the 1840's, it seems that a young gypsy girl, Kati Coch, fell foul not of a ghost, but greed. Stupidly, she stole an extremely valuable — easily identifiable and soon-to-be-missed — silver jug from the dining room at Greenmeadow. She was caught and later hanged on Heath Common (near the present day Gabalfa interchange). Before she died, however, she is said to have cursed Greenmeadow — along with the Lewises, of course — and to have sworn that it would lie in ruins within a hundred years.

Whether she did or whether she didn't — and it does seem a rather apocrophal story — Greenmeadow was indeed in a state of ruin by the time a hundred years had elapsed. The house saw its last great days when owned by Colonel Henry Lewis (1848-1925) — a man remembered, according to his memorial in St Michael's Church, as being 'pleasant in his lifetime', although it seems that this was not how many of the villagers would have described him. He it was who added a single-storey extension to the house for his collection of toby-jugs and other curios, including treasure from Inca tombs. When he died the estate passed to his eldest son, Captain Harry Lewis. The house, however, was closed. From that date on it remained uninhabited. No one was to live there ever again. Moreover, unable to retain it, Captain Lewis began to sell the estate off — a piecemeal process which continued throughout the 1930's.

Greenmeadow gradually declined into being no more than a

derelict, overgrown shell. And then, in May 1940, a fatal accident took place there. It was reported in the *Cardiff and Suburban News* the following day:

> '*Two Killed When Mansion Collapses* — On Thursday part of old Greenmeadow Mansion collapsed with the result that Amram Matthews, caretaker, and Evan Evans, both of Tongwynlais, were killed. The old mansion is well known as the home of the Lewis family but during recent years it has been partly demolished. Complaints have been made that it was a disfigurement, and locals hope that as a result of this tragedy complete demolishing will be decided upon.'

Shortly afterwards the same paper carried an article by Gwen Wyndham Lewis, Henry Lewis' daughter. She wrote: 'Reading of the distressing accidents that happened at my old home, some of your readers may find interest in reading what I know to be true that occurred in this old house.' She confirmed stories of the old Oak Room being haunted and added that in addition to Captain Mostyn a Miss Mary Anne Langley of Green Hill near Cardiff, a Miss Moggridge and a well-known doctor had also seen the 'vision' in the room. She confirmed too both the story told about the Melingriffith Band and the strange death of Greenmeadow's old gardener, Daniel:

> 'Daniel always drove us away when he saw us about the lawn and would never explain the reason. 'Indeed to goodness, keep away, will you?' he used to call out. My many dogs would not remain if I went. These and poor Daniel himself were found lying dead on the very spot he hated one summer's morning.'

Many people, including Lady Beaconsfield (Mrs Wyndham Lewis), she continued, found Greenmeadow a depressing place; oppressive and silent and 'where laughter seemed out of place'. She herself, she said, didn't feel that way about Greenmeadow, but she admitted that she too had had a number of strange experiences there:

'Long years ago, in 1882, I was sent to Greenmeadow with a little friend named Gwyn Thomas, and my dear old nurse, 'Nancy', from 'the Ton', and our well beloved John Palmer, the gamekeeper, was there to take care of us two young folk. My family remained at Weston-super-Mare. That night there was a fearful storm of wind and thunder, and we all huddled together in the hall, close to a roaring log fire, when we were suddenly startled by three loud knocks which vibrated through the house and the front door bell pealed violently. How welcome was John Palmer's kindly face, when he appeared to ascertain what it was all about, and how I admired him when he threw open the door, to show us that no one was there. That, as he expressed it, was those darned rats.

First thing next morning the message arrived informing my father had passed away.'

She concluded by telling how her mother, Sophia Antoinette Timeneas Gwynne, died in poverty in West Kensington in October 1912:

'On October 25th I had left my mother for a brief walk; for years she had suffered from a terrible complaint. Before leaving our little house I had locked the sitting room door, placing the key in my pocket. The room was on the ground floor, no access to the house from the rear. My friend and I returned in ten minutes to find it impossible to re-enter the sitting room, a heavy object was leaning against the door from the inside of the room. After a lot of trouble an entrance was made by the window, and the picture from the wall, of Greenmeadow, measuring seven feet by three feet, was against the door, also a picture of my mother's home, Glanbran, Camarthenshire, making entry impossible. That night three large pictures that I had placed in the small passage fell with a crash, and they consisted of my father's portrait, the Gwynne Coat of Arms, painted on a Hatchment, and another coat of arms picture. None was damaged, and the nails and wires were intact.'

Later that year the 'strange old house', Greenmeadow, was finally demolished.

The following year the *Cardiff and Suburban News* once again carried an article on the ghost stories associated with the house. Once again Gwen Wyndham Lewis got in touch with the paper. On this occasion she sent in a copy of a letter written by Miss Martha Moggridge of Rhiwbina in 1848 and addressed to her father, Henry Lewis. The letter — reproduced here in its entirety — read:

'Dear Squire,

You asked me to inform you to the best of my remembrance of the facts of the visitations, visions, or whatever name it may please you to call it by.

My sister, as your dear wife will remember, was confined to her room, the old oak bedroom over the dining room in your house. I was reading to her as she could not sleep and we were both disturbed by a soft scratching near the door of the room.

My sister suggested it was the cat. I thought maybe it came from rats or mice, but on searching nothing became visible, and I proceeded with the book.

Shortly I noticed my sister was asleep and looking at my watch I noticed the hour was 3 a.m. Fearful to move in case I disturbed my sister I continued my reading and must myself have taken forty winks as something suddenly startled me. My first glance was given to my sister. She lay in bed fully awakened too, and we both stared at the bedroom door which slowly opened and a face with a large prominent nose and a shock of rather white hair peered through the open door.

We could only stare. There was no time for thought, when the door was pushed open, and into our room entered a small old man clad in a green coat and white knee breeches, and I remember I noticed many silver buttons on the coat and much lace hanging from the wrist. Also I noticed a silver rapier hanging from a sash to his side.

On entering the room for a moment he remained

41

stationary, then passed his hands across his eyes in a somewhat perplexed way.

I caught my sister's hand. She was sitting up in bed, and it was she, not I who called out firmly. 'Who are you and what do you want?' As you, Squire, are aware, dear Mabel always boasted of her nerve and self-control. Would I were more akin to her! The figure completely ignored her, and commenced tapping on the walls of the room about I should say a yard or so from the floor.

'Ring the bell very gently,' my sister whispered. Obeying her I gave an over-strong tug to the old tapestry-work rope hanging by the old four poster bed, with the result it dropped useless to the floor. My voice appeared to have left me. I was useless. I could only squeeze my sister's hand who was watching keenly the figure still bent on some search.

Backwards and forwards he moved, always Tap! Tap! I am thankful to say on the opposite side of the room to where we were. Suddenly he threw up his arm with a gesture of great despair and, as still our eyes were on him, vanished, as the saying goes, 'into thin air'.

Both my sister and I were shivering as with extreme cold. I suggested awakening you or dear Sophie. My sister clung to me, begging me not to leave her . . . I hammered with a chair on the floor. I called till my voice gave out. The bell wire I could not reach. My sister I could not leave.

No one but the old house and the watch-dog who answered my frantic calls by a friendly bark could hear me, and to be truthful even if I could have left my sister I dreaded to cross the dark passage to make the sleepers awake.

Dawn came at last. My sister still implored me not to leave though every squeak from the floorboards or unexpected noise made us dread the return of our uninvited visitor. The maid's knock at our door was a never-to-be-forgotten welcome sound.

Almost pushing her aside, I said 'Wait please, with my sister.' I rushed to your bedroom door. I banged. I need not repeat it here. You will so well remember how your dear wife in her corn-red flannel dressing-gown returned with me to my sister with the usual Welsh advice for every ill, 'A nice hot cup of tea.'

As I left your room, Squire, I heard you, you naughty man, chuckling to yourself and saying 'A lot of nonsense! Fiddle-de-dee! Women's imagination!'

Well, Squire, what happened afterwards when we left to come here next day? How about our good Captain Mostyn of the 24th Regiment? What did he tell you, namely that he was awakened at dawn and saw a small old man in old fashioned clothes creeping around tapping the walls of the room he was in, the same bedroom occupied by myself and my sister?

And again that night when the whole house was aroused by the clanking of many footsteps up and down the old stone passages and how John Palmer, your Tongwynlais game-keeper, was aroused, armed with his gun, the terrified maids cowering in the rear, to face the unseen intruder.

Don't talk about 'Women's imaginations' Henry, my dear. To use a sentence of the very long ago: 'There are more things in Heaven and Earth than are dreamt of,' etc.

Our love to you both. Never place me in that room again, tell Sophie.

From yours affectionately,
Martha Moggridge.

Eventually a small council estate was built on the site where Greenmeadow had once stood. The old ghost stories were largely forgotten.

Until 1974.

It was then that a Mrs Suzanne Morgan who lived in a four-bedroom house on the estate with her eight children reported that the ghost of an elderly woman had appeared, on several occasions, in one of the upstairs rooms. In addition, she complained, taps had been turned on in the bathroom while she and her children were asleep, loud banging noises came from the attic which would then immediately be followed by the distinct sound of footsteps and ash from the fireplace was repeatedly raked out onto the carpet overnight. On one occasion, she added, she went to the bathroom to find that it had been locked from the inside. But the incidents didn't end there apparently; they began to increase — both in frequency and in their capacity to frighten and alarm. Chairs, cupboards and sideboards were moved, said Mrs Morgan. And then the figure of the woman appeared on the landing one day and called out 'Julie' — the name of one of her children. Following this latter incident, continued Mrs Morgan, she and her children became too afraid to sleep in any of the upstairs rooms, and took to sleeping downstairs instead.

Mrs Morgan was prescribed tablets for her nerves by her doctor. 'I never used to believe in ghosts until all this started happening,' she told the *Cardiff Leader* which published her story. 'Now I am scared stiff.'

The *Cardiff Leader* decided to investigate Mrs Morgan's story further. They sent a reporter, Bill Corke, and a photographer, Keith Baker, to spend a night in the house. On the chosen night the Morgan family retired to their downstairs beds while the two newspapermen settled down for the night in two armchairs in the main upstairs bedroom.

Nothing happened, it seems, until two in the morning. And then a strange haze seemed to fill the room. At the same time it seemed to grow strangely cold.

In the space of a few moments, however, everything had returned to normal once more.

The following six hours passed without incident. Even so, before leaving the room Keith Baker shot a roll of film — just in case there was something there that remained invisible to the human eye.

When that film came to be developed, it was found to be completely blank. The film, which had been reeled on by the camera quite normally, hadn't been exposed. The camera was examined for faults. There weren't any. The film should have been exposed quite normally. There seemed to be no reason to explain why it shouldn't have been. The two o'clock haze in the room could possibly be explained, sceptics might argue, by the fact that both men smoked. The non-exposure of the film, however, is less easily explained away. Whatever, the paper contacted the *Psychic News* and gave them details both of what Mrs Morgan had told them and of what had occurred when their reporter and photographer visited the house. The *Psychic News* suggested that all of the phenomena could have been caused by the activities of a poltergeist.

One question, of course, remained: could it all have had anything to do with Greenmeadow?

Many locals had no doubt that it had.

Back, now, to Castell Coch.

The castle which originally stood on the site was built by the Normans. By 1540, however, it was described as being 'al in ruine'. The present day castle — just like Cardiff Castle to the south — is a 'gigantic sham, a costly folly', built by William Burgess. It was at the instigation of the third Marquess of Bute that the project was begun: in 1872. It was completed in 1875. Once again (like Cardiff Castle) its style is mock-gothic; romanticised and elaborately stylised. With its tall, conical towers rising above the densely wooded hillside on which it stands, it is an impressive sight — a true fairytale castle.

It was the crumbling, red sandstone ruin of the original, Norman, castle which first had a ghost story associated with it.

It begins with a story of hidden treasure.

In 1858 — almost certainly in an effort to advertise his own business — the Cardiff chemist Robert Drane wrote '*Castel Coch, a gossiping companion to the ruin and its neighbourhood*' and told how a secret treasure was said to have been hidden in an underground passage beneath the castle. He described how a party of 'stout-hearted gentlemen' once decided to explore the underground passage:

> 'So, provided with torches and pickaxes, they set out on their expedition. On and on they went, and at last, shining through the darkness, they saw four bright red lights: very

bright and very red they were. Nothing daunted they advanced, and presently found that the four red lights were the eyes of two huge eagles, who were composedly perched on an IRON CHEST. Now here was confirmation of the legend of Coch Castle! They walked bravely forward, when suddenly the eagles sprang upon them with claw and beak; and very glad they were to make good their retreat, while the royal birds flew back to the chest. But the men were persevering fellows, and the following day returned armed with pistols and eight good bullets, and when they came within proper distance of the eagles they fired, but with no effect; their enemies flew screaming towards them, beat out their torches with their wings, and sent the invaders back crest-fallen. They then cast some silver bullets, and got them duly blessed, and even persuaded a minister with his Holy Book to companion them. Again they saw the four red lights — an exorcism was read, which the eagles did not heed — the charmed bullets were fired with no better result than those of lead — a third assault was made by the eagles upon the disturbers of their watch and attackers of their ward, the enraged birds punishing them more severely than on either of their former visits. It is believed that the eagles are still there, though no one is bold enough to disturb them.'

In 1861, in *The Book of South Wales, the Wye and the Coast*, S.C. and A.M. Hall prefaced Drane's account of hidden treasure at the castle with a story of their own — drawn, it seems, from local tradition. This story has it that a woman of 'good family but small income' once took up residence in ruined castle, having been invited to do so by the then owner and having refurbished a number of the rooms there. With her she brought her two elderly servants: a man and his wife. Shortly after they had moved in, all three began hearing strange noises there. These they put down to rats, mice or birds — nothing more. But then, late one night, the lady awoke to find a man, dressed in the style of a Cavalier, standing in her room staring at her. His face was quite pale, his expression one of grief, sorrow, loss. As the lady sat up in bed he then slipped away into the shadows and disappeared through the door. At once the lady went to follow him. She found that the door was still locked and bolted.

The lady didn't tell her aged servants of her ghostly encounter; they had already become worryingly unnerved by the continuation of strange noises in the castle and had told her that they thought that she — and they — should leave. That evening, returning to her room from a turret garden which she had made, she encountered the figure of the Cavalier for a second time. This time he passed clean through a wall near the garden.

After this the lady began to encounter the ghost quite often, the ghost then usually disappearing by walking through walls or locked doors, just as it had on the first occasion when she had seen it.

Locals, it seemed, had it that the figure was that of the owner of the castle during the Civil War. He had, they said, buried an iron chest full of coins and silver plate in an underground passage which linked the castle to that at Cardiff. Unfortunately for him, however, he had been killed when a petronel (a large calibre firearm often used by cavalry) exploded and he was struck by shrapnel. He had never been able to reclaim his hidden treasure.

In time the lady's servants (who, perhaps, had seen the ghost for themselves) became too afraid to remain at the castle any longer. They left. The lady, preferring to remain with them, left with them.

It is entirely possible, of course, that the story of the Cavalier's hidden treasure arose after these events. Certainly another story did — this harking back to Drane's colourful story. It was said that a hidden treasure at the castle belonged to the Welsh leader Ifor Bach who once scaled the walls of Cardiff Castle under cover of darkness with a number of his men and kidnapped the Earl, his wife and son and then held them captive at Castell Coch until a ransom was paid and his lands restored to him. According to this particular tradition, he was supposed to have had two of his men changed into eagles to guard the treasure. The eagles' capacity for ferocity was said to stem from their intense craving to be made human again.

Another ghost — still said to haunt the castle — is that of 'Poor Dame Griffiths'. Her young son, exploring the ruined castle — sometime in the 17th century, it seems — fell into a deep pool there and drowned. His body was never found. Shortly afterwards his mother died of grief at his death and, the story ends, haunted both the castle and the surrounding woods from then on; still desperately seraching for him.

A final story told about Castell Coch concerns *Mallt y Nos* (Matilda of the Night). A Norman lady of the Conquest period, she is said to have declared, such was her passion for the pursuit: 'If I cannot hunt in Heaven, I would rather not go there'. Her wish was fulfilled. After her death she was, instead, sent to ride for eternity with Arawn, the satanic master of the *Cŵn Annwn* (Dogs of Hell), whose spectral hunt haunted the area around the castle. Her wailing, local tradition had it, could often be heard all over the forest at night.

It is worth noting a few more details about the spectral hunt of which she was said to have become part.

Arawn, the master of the hunt, also known as *Gwyn ap Nudd* (*Gwyn* — the Celtic Lord of the Dead, *ap* — son of, *Nudd* — the chief sky God of the tribes of Ancient Britain), is said to be a dark, towering figure mounted on a huge black horse and carrying a crop of red-hot iron. His hounds — hounds from Hell which, according to tradition, chase the terrified souls of the damned through the skies — are similarly known by a variety of names. They are known as 'Witch Hounds' in Sussex, 'Wisht Hounds' (*Wisht* being a dialect word meaning sad and uncanny) on Dartmoor, 'Yeth Hounds' (*Yeth* meaning heathen) in Devon, 'Gabriel Hounds' in Durham, and as both *Cŵn Annwn* (Dogs of Hell) and *Cŵn y Wybr* (Dogs of the Sky) in South Wales. Together with their master, they are variously known by such names as 'The Devil and his Dandy Dogs' (Cornwall), 'The Wild Hunt' (Germany), 'The Hunt Macabre' (France). As these examples will illustrate, they are a well-known phenomenon not only throughout Britain, but throughout Europe as well.

But fact now takes over from folklore. What the sounds are, in

Tintern Abbey

The Cross Keys Inn, *Usk*

The Queen's Head Inn, *Monmouth*

The Skirrid Inn, *Llanfihangel Crucorney*

Castell Coch

Cardiff Castle

The Cow and Snuffers, *North Llandaff, Cardiff*

The New Theatre, Cardiff

The National Museum, Cardiff

Pwllywrach Manor, nr Colwinston

Sker House

Dunraven Bay

Greenmeadow

Caerphilly Castle

Ogmore Castle

St Donat's Castle

Oystermouth Castle

Penard Castle

Neath Abbey

Ewenny Priory

The Welcome To Town Inn, *Llanrhidian, Gower*

Rhossili Bay, Gower, the Old Rectory the white house on the headland

The Salt House, Port Eynon, Gower

The Captain's Wife, *Sully*

Boverton Castle

Tresillian Cave, Southerndown

fact, are those made by skeins of wild geese making eerie 'yelping' cries while on the wing. Even so, sweeping overhead in such a fashion at night, they have alarmed the superstitious for centuries.

Aside from haunting the area around Castell Coch, Arawn and his hounds are also said to haunt numerous other areas in South Wales.

A third building in Tongwynlais to have had ghost stories told about it is Cilynys farmhouse across the River Taff towards Morganstown, adjoining the Iron Bridge connecting the two settlements.

This story has it that during the Civil War Castell Coch was held by Royalists, but that they were bombarded into submission from the Tynant mount (Ty Nant Moote) by the Roundheads at the suggestion of a local woman. Later the woman was captured by the Royalists and murdered so brutally in a room in Cilynys farmhouse that blood covered all of the walls. To this day, it is said, nothing can conceal the stains. The murdered woman's ghost, meanwhile, is still said to haunt the farmhouse.

Pick up a menu at The Captain's Wife restaurant at Swanbridge and you'll find a brief outline of the story from which the restaurant derives its name.

This is the full story.

Sully House once stood on the site, and at one time during its history was tenanted by a ship's captain. On one of his voyages, the captain took his wife with him aboard his ship. During the voyage, however, she caught a fever and died. The captain, anxious to avoid arousing the superstitions of the crew about having a corpse aboard ship, doubled-up her body and placed it in a lead-lined box in his cabin. For the remainder of the voyage he kept up the pretence that she was still well, despite the fact that, of course, none of the crew ever saw her on deck. Finally, the captain brought his ship back to Sully. He then rowed the box containing his wife's body ashore one night and placed it in the cellar of the house. From there, awaiting a coffin to be delivered, he took the box out into the wood at the back of the house and buried it in a makeshift grave beneath the trees.

There his wife's body lay until a proper coffin was delivered. With the help of the undertaker the captain then carried the coffin out into the wood and began to dig.

The grave was empty. The box and the body of his wife had been removed. It was later assumed that a member of the captain's crew had seen him row the box ashore and, having decided that it contained some sort of treasure, decided to steal it — so had kept watch on him while he had buried it in the wood.

The captain, utterly distraught at what had happened, died shortly afterwards.

And it was then that stories began to circulate in the area that Sully House and the wood behind it were haunted by the ghost of his dead wife, cruelly denied a christian burial. Many people claimed to have seen her — sometimes dressed all in black, sometimes dressed all in white — moving between the wood and the house. Some years later the then tenant of the house was awoken by one of her maids who claimed that she had seen the ghost of the captain's wife standing by her bedside. The maid, it seems, was so frightened that she gave up her job; too afraid to spend another night in the house.

In around 1870 some repairs were being made to the stables adjoining the house. Some of the flagstones in the yard there were taken up during the course of the work and beneath them a skeleton was discovered: the remains of the captain's wife. It was decided that whoever had removed her body from the wood had hidden it there and had kept the box in which she had been buried for the sake of its lead-lining.

There is, however, another version of the story, recorded in a series of articles in the *Penarth Times* in 1925.

This has it that towards the end of the 18th century Sully House was occupied by a Colonel Rhys, who had then recently retired from the army. Across the Severn Estuary in Bristol, meanwhile, a young woman and a young ship's captain by the name of Henry Winstanley had fallen in love with one another. The young woman's father strongly disapproved of the relationship, however. He took drastic measures to end it. He arranged with the owners of Winstanley's ship to have the latter sent on a voyage to Jamaica and then, while he was away, married his daughter off to Colonel Rhys.

Eventually, Winstanley returned to Bristol. When he learned what had happened in his absence, he at once took his ship across to Sully, having first of all arranged with his lover that he would anchor off Sully Island one night and at an agreed signal row ashore and collect her so that they could run away together.

Everything seemed to go according to plan. On the night in question the Colonel's wife appeared on the lawn in front of Sully House waving a white handkerchief to let Winstanley know that all was clear and that it was safe for him to come ashore. Unfortunately, she was wrong. Far from being well out of the way, her husband — having learned of her tryst with Winstanley — was lying in wait in the wood behind the house. No sooner had Winstanley rowed ashore and made his way up onto the lawn, then, than the Colonel ran out to attack him, his sword at the ready.

The two men were soon locked in a vicious sword-fight. Momentarily distracted by his young wife throwing a scarf at him, the Colonel was then run through by the younger man's sword. He fell to the ground, dying.

As he died he pronounced what for someone in his condition is an impressively prolix curse:

> 'May heaven's vengeance rest upon you for all time. May the remembrance of this day's deed never be absent from your thoughts, waking or sleeping, and as often as yon moon shines upon the scene wherever your bones may be at the time, living or dead, may your spirit be forced to return to this spot and again enact this deed.'

Winstanley buried the Colonel's body beneath some shrubbery and then rowed back to his ship with his lover, now the Colonel's widow.

Naturally, the disappearance of the Colonel and his wife was the subject of much speculation in the village. It was finally assumed, however, that they had both been kidnapped by pirates; Sully being well known for being frequented by such brigands. As to Winstanley and the Colonel's widow, meanwhile: bad luck, it seemed, sailed with them away from Sully. The ship's crew became restless with a woman aboard and, in a distant port, deserted. A second crew then mutinied as the ship began its homeward journey and brought to ship back to Sully. There — again, off Sully Island — they locked the two lovers into their cabin and, for some reason, set the ship ablaze. Winstanley and the Colonel's widow perished in the flames.

Thereafter the ghost of the Colonel's widow — sometimes dressed all in black, sometimes dressed all in white (echoing what was said about the captain's wife) — was said to haunt Sully House, usually appearing there at midnight three days before a full moon. Villagers claimed that candles could be seen flickering in the windows of the empty house, that screams and shouts could be heard there — and, on occasions, the clash of swords too: a ghostly re-enactment of the fatal sword-fight between Colonel Rhys and Captain Winstanley.

At Llanvithyn, north of the village of Llancarfan, there was once a monastery. At some point or other during its history, according to legend, a man sought sanctuary there, hoping to avoid his enemies. The monks duly took him in. Their protection, it seems, wasn't enough. The man was caught by whoever it was he was trying so desperately to escape, had part of his leg hacked off (why, no one knows) and was then bricked up in a wall to die. It is worth noting at this point, however, that 'walling-up' was a punishment often meted out by monks themselves whenever they caught hold of anyone who they deemed to have transgressed against them, against God or whoever. Perhaps they hadn't afforded their 'guest' any protection at all? Whatever, centuries later alterations were carried out at the monastery and — in a cavity in a wall — a skeleton was discovered. The lower half of one of the legs was missing. That said, it wasn't the ghost of this unfortunate who was reputed to haunt the site of the monastery in later years; it was the ghost of his wife — another ghost to become known as the Lady in White.

At nearby Bonvilston, Cottrell Manor House is said to be haunted by one Emilia Gwenneth, while at Duffryn House at St Nicholas, further to the east, the ghost of Admiral Sir Thomas Button is said to haunt both the cellar of the house and the grounds there. Famous both as an Arctic explorer and for his successes against pirates operating along the South Glamorgan coast, he is said to appear most frequently in the grounds — usually on windy nights for some reason.

Moving west again, the Pant-yr-Ysgyrd bridge at the market town of Cowbridge is known locally as the 'Spirits' Bridge' — this because it is held to be haunted by the ghosts of a woman and child (although it is also said that the ghost of a clergyman has been seen there too). The woman is thought to have been the wife of a local landowner whose wont it was to violently mistreat her — and who ended up murdering her. Exactly when this took place and how the child came to be involved isn't known, but it seems that at some point in time some men quarrying beneath the bridge found the skeletons of a woman and child buried there. On the woman's wrist was an iron ring.

In the 19th century it was said that Caercady House, situated midway between Welsh St Donat's and the hamlet of Prisk, was haunted. The family who lived there at the time told of knocking sounds under the floors, of the sounds of rustling dresses and the tread of heavy footsteps on the stairs having been heard there. A rather more curious sound which they had heard they likened to that of a box of books being dropped onto the floor, the books then scattering in all directions. There were also repeated knocks at both the front and back doors, they complained. Eventually they grew so tired of these (answering the door at which they had heard the knocks only to find that there was no one there) that they simply ignored them. Then, one evening, they saw a 'shadowy being clad in grey' flit past one of the windows, a look of disappointment on its face. The family thereafter referred to the ghost with which they seemed to be sharing the house as the Grey Man. They even, it seems, grew rather fond of him.

Remaining with this particular story for a moment, there is a further anecdote told about the house which details how a servant boy from a neighbouring farm once tried to use the Grey Man to his own advantage. Visiting Caercady House one evening for an assignation with one of the maids in an upstairs room there — which the family didn't use — he tapped on the walls and floor in a mischevious attempt to scare off any the servants in that part of the house. Unfortunately for him another visitor to the house — a farmer's wife — heard the sounds and wasn't at all put off by the thought that it was the Grey man who was responsible for them. Quite the reverse; she decided to investigate in the hope of seeing the ghost for herself. What she found when she burst into the room, of course, was rather different from any ghostly activity which she might have expected to find there.

At Llanblethian a ghost was once said to haunt a lane in the village — Heol Y Felin. It was thought to be that of a Scottish packman who was murdered there in 1760 and whose murderers buried his body in a makeshift grave beside the lane. His remains were discovered in 1840 when a local farmer incorporated the lane (by then disused) into one of his fields.

Also at Llanblethian, of course, there was once the house said to have been haunted by the ghost which inspired the verses which precede this selection of stories from South Glamorgan.

Near St Athan is the site of West Norchéte (West Orchard) Castle. In the Norman era it seems that this was owned by one Sir William Berkerolles who was married to the daughter of the Lord of Glamorgan, the Lady de Clare.

Sir William took part in the second crusade to the Holy Land and it was upon his return, according to legend, that he accused his wife of having been unfaithful to him during his absence. Lady de Clare swore that she was innocent, but Sir William refused to listen; even citing one Sir Gilbert D'Umphreville (of East Norchéte Castle) as her lover. He then took it upon himself to exact his revenge. To begin with, then, he locked her into her room to starve. The servants, however, undermined his plan by surreptitiously bringing her food. Sir William then seized upon a delightful custom which he had learned from the Saracens: he had her buried up to her neck in a field near the castle. He issued instructions that no one was to go near her; she was to be left to die there. At which point Lady de Clare's sister intervened. But to no avail. Sir William was adamant: that his wife had betrayed him, that she would die for having done so in the manner he had prescribed. Promising that she would take neither food nor water to her, Lady de Clare's sister was allowed only the minor concession of being able to visit her once a day, early each morning. Even so, in a desperate effort to at least ease her sister's suffering, she put her visits to as much use as she possibly could. As she walked out into the field each morning she would make sure that the hem of her dress trailed in the dew until it was soaked. She would then have her sister suck it so that she could have something to drink — and while she herself couldn't be accused by Sir William of having broken her promise to him.

After being left out in the field for ten days, however, Lady de Clare died, of hunger, cold and exhaustion.

A year later Sir William learned that she was innocent of all he had accused her of, that he had been duped into believing that she had been unfaithful to him. She had been telling him the truth when she had denied that she had committed adultery during his years away from home. What had happened, instead, during that time was that Sir Gilbert D'Umphreville had tried to persuade her to run away with him. She had refused him. Humiliated, Sir Gilbert had then put about the rumour that they had been lovers in order to exact his revenge upon her — knowing what her husband's reaction would be once he returned from the Holy Land. And he hadn't been wrong; Sir William had behaved as brutally, as boorishly and as stupidly as his callous and calculating neighbour had predicted.

Overcome with both grief and guilt, Sir William took to drink. He shut himself away in his rooms for days on end where he would then beat the walls and shout for his wife to come back to him, to forgive him for what he had done.

Surprisingly, however, it was neither Sir William nor his

woefully wronged wife who came to haunt East Norchéte; it was Lady de Clare's sister. She is said to have been seen on frequent occasions over the years: a figure in white sometimes seen walking across the field where Lady de Clare is thought to have died (near the road to 'Bats Leys'), sometimes seen walking in a slow circle around a certain spot there. She is known, almost inevitably, as the White Lady — Y Ladi Wen. On each occasion when she has been seen it has, it seems, been at around early dawn.

The remains of Boverton Castle, meanwhile, are said to be haunted by a Lady in Black. She is said to walk slowly within its walls, often sobbing as she does so.

Tradition has it that she is the ghost of Hadwisa, the daughter of the Earl of Gloucester who owned the castle (which she later inherited) and the first wife of Richard I's infamous younger brother, Prince John. John divorced her in 1200 on the grounds that she couldn't bear him any children. A second — and, it seems, rather more truthful — reason was simply that, as soon as he succeeded to the throne, he decided that he wanted to marry Isabella of Angouleme. Hadwisa was heartbroken and returned to Boverton in despair — where she then remained from then on, a virtual recluse. Even so, it was to Hadwisa that John turned for help when he was on the run from his barons who were pressing him to sign the Magna Carta. She didn't let him down. Taking pity on him, she took him in; disguising him as a servant. He remained with her at Boverton for six months.

When the castle was being dismantled early in the 19th century, workmen claimed that they had seen a ghost — dressed in black (as though in mourning), tall and with long dark hair reaching down to her waist — walking through the ruins on several occasions. On other occasions, they said, they had heard the distinct sound of the female phantom weeping somewhere nearby even though they couldn't actually see her anywhere. An old lady in the village informed them that they had seen (and heard) 'Wissie' and added that she too had seen her ghost on a number of occasions.

Why 'Wissie' should appear to be so distressed on those occasions when she is seen or heard at the castle isn't known but, of course, it has been suggested that she is still in 'mourning' for having been so cruelly abandoned by Prince John in favour of another woman.

It is another Lady in White who is said to have been seen just outside the village of Llanmaes north of Boverton. On the road leading out of the village towards Llantwit Major is the site of a well once known as the White Pool. Nearby is Eagle Well Road which leads to where the Hangman's Tree once stood. The Lady in White is said to walk between the site of the well and the site of the tree.

Eagle Well Road, meanwhile, is said to have ghosts all of its own. It is said that the ghosts of people hanged at the Hangman's Tree have been seen here, slowly making their way towards the place where they met their death at the end of the hangman's rope. The road, it seems, is also known locally by another name, a grim reminder of its past: Gallows Walk. At the site of the actual tree ghostly thuds are said to have been heard.

Two buildings which once stood opposite one another on the road are also said to have been haunted. One was the disused Bethesda chapel (reputed to glow with a ghostly blue light on certain nights), the other a house named Froglands.

At Llantwit Major itself are the ruins of Old Place (also known as Llantwit Place or Llantwit Castle). These are said to be haunted by the ghost of a woman who was starved to death by her husband, a former owner of the house. Some versions of the story have it that he also starved their only child to death at the same time.

A second story from the village is that of the 'Frampton Horse', a story which has its origins at the opposite end of the country, in North Wales.

In 1282, according to this story, Llywelyn ap Gruffydd (the last truly Welsh Prince of Wales) moved South with his army, leaving his brother to continue the Welsh campaign against Edward I in the North. At Builth Wells, however, he was defeated by the English and was forced to flee for his life. Together with his squire he hid in a ditch on the banks of the River Irfon. According to some sources, he was badly wounded. Whatever, it seems that he and his squire were discovered there by two passing knights, John Gifford and Edmund Mortimer. They killed the squire and then the unarmed Llywelyn. They then decapitated the Welsh Prince, washed his head in the cold water of the river and carried it to Edward at Rhuddlan Castle (from where it would later be taken to be displayed at the gates to the city of Chester.)

Overcome with remorse for having shamed his knighthood by killing two unarmed men, it seems that one of the two knights who had ended Llywelyn's life retired to Llantwit Major, to two properties which he owned there: Great Frampton and Little Frampton. (Some versions of the story have it that he actually changed his name to Frampton, named his properties accordingly.) He then spent much of his time indulging in wild cross-country rides. And it was this which eventually led to his death. Near the gates to Great Frampton he was thrown from his horse and broke his neck. Thereafter, concludes this local legend, the ghosts of both rider and horse were sometimes seen at the scene of the accident. Sometimes — although nothing was actually seen — the sound of a horse galloping along the road was heard, to be followed by the sound of something heavy falling to the ground. Locals habitually avoided the area late at night; terrified of encountering the 'Frampton Horse' for themselves.

Also at Llantwit Major: the ghost of a woman was once said to appear at midnight near the old Roman road. Locals had it that the haunting was connected with the disappearance of a woman in the area some years earlier, when the concensus of opinion was that she had been 'done away with'. Eventually, when the road was being widened, this view was given further credence by the discovery of a skeleton buried there. The remains were duly reinterred in consecrated ground. The woman's ghost, it seems, was never seen again.

The ghost of a large man dressed entirely in black is said to have haunted a field near the gates to Great Frampton. He is reputed to have carried a pitchfork with which he threw burning hay around the field. By a wall next to the gates a large red-eyed dog is said to have appeared on occasion, rattling the heavy chain by which it was secured.

Two final stories concern St Iltyd's church. It was once believed that if anyone looked through the keyhole there on the nights of All Saints, Christmas Eve or New Year, they would be able to see the apparitions of all those in the village who would die within the next twelve months. It was also said that the sounds of digging could sometimes be heard in the graveyard — a phenomenon which was taken to presage the death of a prominent member of the community within the following few days.

St Donat's Castle, now part of an international sixth-form boarding school, Atlantic College, stands on the coast just beyond Llantwit Major. Many parts of the building date back to the 14th century. For hundreds of years it was the home of the Stradling family. It also had the reputation of being one of the most haunted houses in the whole of Wales.

The most famous ghost said to haunt the castle is that of Lady Anne Stradling who, legend has it, was murdered here and after whom the Lady Anne Tower (now the headmaster's residence) is named. Leading from the tower — and overlooking the terraced gardens, the school's outdoor swimming pool and the Bristol Channel beyond — is the Long Gallery. It is here that Lady Anne's ghost is supposed to walk, in 'trailing silks and tapping high heel shoes'. It is further said that she is waiting there (looking out to sea) for her husband to return from a pilgrimage to the Holy Land — the story here being that he never did, having been killed in a duel in Italy.

Lady Anne's appearances — which would prompt all of the hounds at the castle to bay and howl — were held to presage either a death in the Stradling family or some misfortune which was about to befall it. There is a story that her ghost appeared in 1449, shortly before Henry Stradling, the son of the then owner of the castle, Edward Stradling, was kidnapped while sailing home to St Donat's from Somerset. His kidnapper was the (improbably named) Breton pirate Colyn Dolphyn who was, apparently, well known for frequenting this particular part of the South Wales coastline.

The story of the kidnapping is interesting, too, in that it leads on to another ghost story associated with the castle.

According to this story, Henry Stradling was released after a ransom was paid, but thereafter swore to gain revenge on Dolphyn some day. And so he did. When, four years later, he inherited the castle on the death of his father, he had a watchtower built on the cliffs and had a lookout posted there at all times to search the horizon for Dolphyn's ship. Dolphyn, it seems, was eventually lured onto the rocks beneath the cliff by a false light in the tower when he showed up on one occasion — and it was then that Henry Stradling exacted his revenge in no small measure. Captured, Dolphyn was taken to Tresillian Cave (also known as the Cave of the Celtic Venus and the scene of many clandestine marriages), bound hand and foot and buried up to his neck in the wet sand at the cave's entrance. There he was left to drown. His screams as the tide came in are still said to be heard in the cave — albeit faintly — on New Year's Eve.

A second version of the story exists, however. This simply has it that Dolphyn was hanged at the castle after he was captured — either from a tree in the grounds or on Castle Tower, then known as Gibbet Tower.

Mallt y Nos (Matilda of the Night) has already been mentioned in connection with Castell Coch. She is said to haunt St Donat's Castle too; appearing once a year — usually on stormy nights, dressed in a hooded cloak — to then hunt for the soul of Colyn Dolphyn. Villagers apparently got in on the act too in the past. For years they took to burning effigies of the pirate in commemoration of his association with the area.

In his *Ghost Book* (1937), Lord Halifax records an account of an exorcism supposedly carried out at the castle by a well-known spiritualist (whose identity he declined to divulge). The account was sent to him by a Charles G. Sterling who had met the spiritualist while staying in Scotland in 1917.

It reads as follows:

> 'For some time the inhabitants of St Donat's Castle had been greatly alarmed by a variety of ghostly phenomena which appeared by day as well as by night. The materialisations which occurred, scared not only the servants and the children

of the house, but also the owner and his wife. The situation at length became so intolerable that the owner, a retired naval officer, decided to let or sell the place, which accordingly was advertised in Country Life.

At this juncture, however, he happened to hear of the fame of Mr X . . . as an exorcist. Mr X . . . is a remarkable man, born in one of the Dominions, who at the age of fourteen discovered that he possessed extraordinary powers of healing. His record of cases is amazing. He devotes his life to healing the sick, and to casting out evil spirits from individuals and from haunted houses.

Informed of Mr X . . . 's gifts, the owner of St Donat's wrote to him, and invited him to pay a visit to the Castle and investigate the phenomena which were giving such trouble. Mr X . . . consented, and in due course arrived. He found that the principal manifestations were as follows:

(1) A panther was repeatedly seen in the corridors by the household.

(2) A bright light, having the semblance of a large, glaring eye, appeared nightly in one of the bedrooms.

(4) The piano, even when closed, was played by invisible hands.

Having received this account of the manifestations, Mr X . . . retired to the bedroom, in which the light had been reported, to pray and grapple with the Powers of Darkness. He requested the owner of the house to sit meanwhile in the hall, with the front door wide open, while the process of exorcism went on. After a while, as though to mark Mr X . . . 's triumph over the evil forces of the place, a great gust of wind suddenly blew out from the room where he was praying, swept down the main staircase, and all but carried the owner of the Castle out into the garden.

From that day and hour, the ghostly disturbances completely ceased. All was peaceful in the Castle, which is no longer to be let or sold.'

But in 1925 it was sold. It was bought by the American

newspaper magnate William Randolph Hearst, who then frequently lived there with the filmstar Marion Davies. He had much of the castle restored — including Lady Anne's Tower.

He also discovered that, apparently, the castle still had ghosts in residence. Locals still spoke of Lady Anne having been seen there and his armourer, Raymond Bartell, who slept in the Castle Tower (Gibbet Tower), claimed to have seen the ghost of Colyn Dolphyn there on several occasions. Eventually the latter took to sleeping with a revolver beneath his pillow.

And the castle is still thought to be haunted. Staff at Atlantic College have reportedly spoken of sensing a 'presence' there, of doors opening and closing by themselves and sporadic outbreaks of what has been assumed to have been poltergeist activity. Often, it seems, wailing sounds have been heard in the castle too.

Finally, to round off this selection of stories from South Glamorgan, it is said that a ghostly pack of hounds can still be heard baying at midnight on August Bank holidays at Pwllywrach (Witches' Well) Manor at Colwinston.

The story attached to this particular phenomenon has it that many years ago a huntsman in charge of the kennels at the house went off and got drunk for several days — completely forgetting about the dogs in his care which had been left locked into the kennels without any food whatsoever. When, at last, he returned, the starving animals savaged him to death as soon as he opened the kennel door.

Given that the story concerns hounds, the Cŵn Annwn get a look in too. A second version of the story simply has it that it is they who can be heard baying at Pwllywrach Manor.

. . . I picked my way, by the light of the full clear moon, towards the old Sker-Grange, which stands a little back from the ridge of the beach, and on the edge of the sand-hills.

This always was, and always must be, a very sad and lonesome place, close to a desolate waste of sand, and the continual roaring of the sea upon black rocks. A great grey house, with many chimneys, many gables, and many windows, yet not a neighbour to look out on, not a tree to feed its chimneys, scarce a firelight in its gable in the very depth of winter. Of course, it is said to be haunted.

(From *The Maid of Sker*, R. D. Blackmore)

Mid Glamorgan

Mid Glamorgan has far fewer ghost stories than might be expected of a county of its size and population — and many of the stories which it does have, moreover, are extremely slight, with few worthwhile details to be had on any of them.

Into this latter category fall four stories to be found just inside the county's boundary north of Cardiff.

To the east, there is the picturesque stately home of Cefn Mably (Mabel's Ridge), now Cefn Mably Hospital. Tradition has it that it was built by Mabel Fitzhamon, the daughter and only child of Robert Fitzhamon who built Newport Castle — and who, of course, is now said to haunt it. During the Civil War the house was owned (as it was from 1447 until its conversion into a hospital in 1920, in fact) by the Kemeys family, who were then staunchly Royalist. Tradition also has it that both the King's Room (so named because Charles I once slept there) and the Bishop's Room (named after the King's travelling companion, Bishop Compton) in the house are haunted — both, it seems, by ghosts thought to date from that turbulent period.

At Taffs-Well a Lady in Grey is said to haunt the riverbank near the well famous for its putative healing powers and from which the village derives its name. At Garth Mountain there is supposed to be a Green Lady thought to be guarding a hidden treasure there, while further west at Creigau an old house in the village known as Castell Mynach is said to be haunted by a White Lady.

Caerphilly is justly renown for its castle. Built in the 13th century by Gilbert de Clare, the 'Red Earl', it remains remarkably intact. It is also reputed to be haunted: primarily by the Earl's French wife, Alice. Gilbert discovered that she had had an affair and banished her to France where she then remained until her death.

Another of the de Clares is said to haunt the castle ramparts and to have been seen there dressed in a full suit of armour. And then there is the *Gwrach y Rhibyn* said to haunt the castle: she is said to have red eyes, a large head, to wear close-fitting green clothes and a green cape and to flap her way around the castle walls after emerging from the waters of the moat.

At Cilfynydd a White Lady riding a phantom white horse is said to haunt the woods near Cwmheldeg, her appearances (which, reportedly, have been witnessed on a number of occasions over the years) supposedly presaging either death or disaster. She is, for instance, said to have appeared before the outbreak of both world wars. Cilfynydd Common, meanwhile, is said to be haunted by the 'Lady of the Common', thought to be the ghost of a woman who was married to a local coal-owner sometime in the 19th century.

Further north still, the Black Pool near Merthyr Tydfil is said to be haunted by the malevolent ghost of a beautiful young woman dressed in flowing white clothes. Tradition has it that she attempts to lure people towards the Black Pool in the hope that they will drown there.

Mountain Ash boasts the legend of Guto Nyth Brân.

Born in 1700 on the remote farm of Nyth Brân (the Crow or Raven's Nest) from which he took his name, Guto made a reputation for himself through his prowess at running. He beat everyone who decided to take him on and race him over the local hills, his neighbours often making easy money by betting on him to do so.

And then, in 1737, Guto took on an equally renowned English runner. Guto won the race, but the race was so hard, had taken such a toll on him, that he later died of exhaustion. His gravestone in the churchyard of St Gwynno's, tucked away in the mountains where he ran, records that he ran 'twelve miles in seven minutes under the hour'. It is also inscribed with a heart — possibly, say some, to commemorate the affection in which he was held, while others suggest that it merely recalls that it was his heart which finally failed him.

On certain occasions Guto's ghost is now said to run across the mountains at midnight.

It is still a tradition in the area that at Mountain Ash's Nos Galan

Races, held on New Year's Eve, a runner dressed as Guto will run down from Llanwynno Church and into the town carrying a blazing torch.

The village of Llangynwyd lies just south of Maesteg near Mid Glamorgan's boundary with West Glamorgan.

Here, tradition has it that in the late 18th century Pentre Farm had a ghost haunting it: a ghost with a grievance.

The story begins that one winter an old pauper, one Philip Thomas, was given permission to sleep in an outhouse by the then owner of the farm. However, it seems that one of the maids at the farm, Catherine, took exception to him and began goading him whenever the opportunity arose. And she didn't stop there — she even complained to her employer that he pestered her in an attempt to have him turned out onto the road again.

And then one day she found the old man dying in the outhouse, having collapsed on the floor there. He begged her for a cup of water. In keeping with her treatment of him since he had arrived at the farm, she refused to bring him one.

The old man then died.

Catherine may well have come to regret her actions unaided, but it seems that Thomas' ghost gave her added cause to do so; disturbing her equilibrium if not her conscience. Catherine often felt his ghost snatching at her clothes, jostling her . . . even slapping her. On one occasion the old man's vengeful spirit threw a bucket of water over her.

Eventually — after the old man's ghost took to throwing stones around the farm and the farmhouse — the farmer called in the local vicar, the Rev. Parry, to exorcise the ghost. However, the Rev. Parry failed to do so. When he was told that Thomas' ghost was standing behind him, he actually fled the farm altogether.

The farmer then called in the Rev. Jones of Glynogwr, who was, apparently, rather more experienced in such matters.

Philip Thomas' ghost was duly exorcised from Pentre Farm.

A second story from the village concerns the Old Vicarage (which was once, presumably, occupied by the Rev. Parry). This is said to harbour a strange 'presence'. Unexplained music is said to have been heard coming from the house and a number of people have reportedly complained both of a feeling of being watched there and of an 'eerie coldness'.

The remainder of Mid Glamorgan's ghost stories are all to be found on its — seemingly placatory — share of the Glamorganshire coastline: at Sker House near Kenfig, at Nottage, Ogmore, Ewenny and Southerndown.

Sker House has been empty since 1969 and currently stands a derelict — and rapidly deteriorating — shell at the southern end of the impressive and expansive sand-dunes of Kenfig Burrows. Despite the proximity of Port Talbot and its imposing steelworks (one of the fascinations of South Wales lies in its frequent cheek-by-jowl juxtaposition of the industrially scarred and the naturally spectacular), it isn't difficult to imagine how it must have looked in its heyday; standing in impressive isolation on this windswept stretch of coast. Certainly, it inspired the author R.D. Blackmore (the author, of course, of *Lorna Doone*) — and it is his novel *The Maid of Sker* which provides the excerpt which precedes this chapter.

The house is mainly of 16th century origin and occupies the site of a grange of Neath Abbey. Built in 1554 by Christopher Tuberville, it remained in the Tuberville family for several generations. It was then occupied by a succession of tenant farmers (who must have found its sheer size somewhat oppressive; the dining hall of the house, for instance, was intended to seat over a hundred people). It was largely due to this that the house escaped any major redevelopment and remains such an impressive example of such a 16th century house of its type — but is also one of the main reasons behind its decline; few repairs were carried out there either. At the time of writing its future looks bleak.

The ghost story told most frequently about Sker House concerns one Elizabeth William (*the* 'Maid of Sker') who is said to have died here in 1776. Tradition has it that she was imprisoned in an upstairs room by her father, who was determined to prevent her from meeting her lover against his wishes. It is in this room that her ghost is reputed to appear — such appearances often accompanied by the clanking of chains (with which her tyrannical father restrained her).

But there are other ghost stories told about the house too. A ghostly white horse was once said to haunt the area, it seems — which, if seen on the night of a full moon, was supposed to give warning of a death. There were also stories both of a strange white light having been seen hovering above Sker and Tusker Rocks and of a 'ghost-ship' having been sighted out to sea there.

And then there is a tale concerning a *toili*. This has it that a man walking along the beach one moonlit night saw, in the distance, the wreck of a large ship breaking up on the rocks. A party of men waded out of the sea, huge waves crashing all around them, carrying something seemingly rather heavy between them. They then headed towards Porthcawl. The man followed them. The men walked to his house, approached the door — and then disappeared. A week later a large ship was wrecked on the rocks, exactly where the man had seen the 'forewarning' of the incident. Many lives were lost. Among the dead was the man's brother, who had been on his way home after many years at sea. His body was carried from the beach by some of his shipmates and taken to his brother's house.

At the village of Nottage, just north of Porthcawl, West Road is said to be haunted by the ghost of a monk wearing a black habit. His appearances are thought to come to an end when he reaches the crossroads, which was supposedly once the site of a gibbet. Because of this, it has been suggested that the monk was possibly martyred — and swung from the gibbet himself.

In the 18th century, according to another story from the area, a waggoner was making his way towards Porthcawl one night during a violent storm. He was advised not to cross the River Ogmore, but did so. He, his wagon and his horses were all washed out to sea. At Merthyr Mawr, where the incident took place, they are now said to reappear on certain occasions when the sea is similarly treacherous.

The sand-dunes at Merthyr Mawr also form the backdrop to

Ogmore Castle on the river Ewenny. Guarding a ford across the river (now marked by stepping stones), the remains of this Norman castle are said to be haunted by a number of restless spirits who, in turn, guard a hoard of gold and silver coins which is buried somewhere nearby.

A second story concerning Ogmore has it that a ghostly female form known as the 'Lady of the Moors' walks to the castle from the site of a hanging tree situated on a hill on the road between Colwinston and Wick, just inside the South Glamorgan boundary.

At Ewenny the ruins of the 12th century priory are said to be haunted by one Ewens, a monk murdered there by a Norman baron. The church at the priory is said to exude a sense of evil. The ruins are said to have a 'depressing, forbidding atmosphere'.

Near Southerndown stood Dunraven Castle, the seat of the successive families of Butler, Vaughan and Wyndham. It was the Butlers who built the original castle sometime in the 12th century. Later, this was incorporated into a house which was built around it. This, in turn, seems then to have been incorporated into a large, Gothic-style castellated mansion which succeeded it in the early 19th century. In 1962 it was demolished.

In the late 17th century it seems that the Vaughan's fell on somewhat hard times. It was then that they took to wrecking. In the 18th century the then owner of Dunraven Castle, Walter Vaughan, was known as the 'wrecker lord'. So successful was he in luring ships onto the rocks around Southerndown that locals claimed that he was in league with the devil. Certainly, Vaughan must have been an evil character; he had his men strip drowned sailors not only of any valuables, but of their clothes as well. Survivors of the wrecks — if there were any — were murdered as soon as they were found.

Vaughan had a son (his only child) who was being educated on the continent. For the latter's twenty first birthday, however, it was planned that he would return to Dunraven Castle for a lavish celebration. His father duly set about luring yet another ship onto the rocks to pay for it. It was November. The sea was often rough and opportunities abounded. Soon a ship was lured onto the rocks at Witches Point. There were no survivors.

As usual, Vaughan and his men set about robbing the bodies which were washed up onto the beach. But then, on one of the corpses, one of his men discovered a ring decorated with the Vaughan's family crest, instantly recognisable and meaning only one thing: the 'wrecker lord' had caused his own son to be drowned.

Vaughan was devastated. He took to drinking more and more heavily. He took to roaming the beach where his son had been found, ranting and raving. Finally, he threw himself into the sea. He too was drowned.

He is said to haunt the beach still.

Dunraven Castle itself was once haunted, it seems, by the ghost of a 'Blue Lady' who always left a distinct smell of mimosa behind her following her appearances there. During the First World War the house was used as a convalescent hospital by the Red Cross and, apparently, the ghost was seen quite often. A nursing sister who arrived at the house in April 1917 was sleep one night in the Amber Room, a room situated on the second floor and overlooking the drive, when it seems that she was awoken by a slight rustling sound and a draught on her face. She was about to get out of bed and close the window in the room, the story continues, when she saw a small female figure wearing a light coloured garment of some sort walk slowly from the doorway to the fireplace. The nurse immediately turned on a light. There was no sign of the figure. The room, however, was filled with the smell of mimosa. That August the nurse saw the Blue Lady for a second time. Switching off her bedside lamp after reading in bed late at night, she suddenly noticed that the room was once again filled with the smell of mimosa. Almost at once she then saw the Blue Lady sitting in a chair by the fireplace. The nurse ran straight to a friend's room and stayed with her the night. Other nurses who stayed in the Amber Room, conclude reports of the haunting, also saw the Blue Lady there, also smelled the scent of mimosa.

Linger with me this olden land to spy:
A land of sleepy hollows, hemmed with woods
And hill-slopes dense with deep-roof'd solitudes;
Of wind-racked moors o'er which the curlews cry,
And the red waves of rolling gorse-fires fly;
Of capes and scaurs, sea-hewn in stormiest moods,
And roaring caves, that nurse the kestrel broods,
Where once old-world carnivora crawled to die.

A land whereupon the breath of Arthur's praise
Floats like a mist; around whose rock-bound coast
Lie Philip's galleons rooted fast in sand,
Hovers in storm-time many a drowned ghost;
A shore for song, a land of yesterdays:
Linger with me about this haunted land.

(*Gower: A Land of Yesterdays*, James Chapman Woods)

West Glamorgan

We begin this selection of stories from West Glamorgan at the easternmost community in the county: Glyncorrwg.

Set at the head of its own remote valley north of Maesteg, Glyncorrwg has two ghost stories to be told about it. One concerns the alleaged haunting of a bakery which once stood there, the other Glyncorrwg colliery.

During the depression of the 1930's, begins the first story, an unemployed baker from Llangollen in North Wales moved south to take up a job in Glyncorrwg bakery. Within a matter of days he had returned home. He was threatened with having his unemployment benefit withdrawn from him and duly appeared before the Court of References at Wrexham. There, he explained his reasons for leaving. On only his second night at the bakery, he said, he heard a repeated tapping sound at the window shortly after midnight. When he went outside to see who or what was causing it, the sound ceased. No sooner had he started work again, however, than — once again — it resumed. The 'tapping' at the window went on for about an hour. The following night, he went on, he felt a sudden draught while he was at work — as though someone had walked past him. But it was on his fourth night at the bakery, he complained, that the most dramatic incident took place: an incident which confirmed his suspicions that the building was haunted. Hearing noises in the room adjoining the bakehouse, he opened the door to investigate. He found himself confronted by the ghost of an elderly woman wearing a black dress. The figure drifted into the bakehouse, looked at him for a moment — and then disappeared. It was then that he decided to leave Glyncorrwg and return to Llangollen.

The baker might have expected to have been laughed out of court. He wasn't; his testimony was supported by a statement from the owner of the bakery which revealed that over the years several workers there had reported similar experiences. They too, it seemed, had heard strange noises while working in the bakery late at night. They too had seen the ghost of the old lady.

The baker's unemployment benefit was only withdrawn from him for a week.

The ghost at Glyncorrwg colliery was said to be a woman in white. Sight or sound of her was believed to forewarn of an impending disaster there. In July 1902, accordingly, over three hundred miners at the colliery refused to work after she was reportedly seen in one of the remote tunnels waving her arms above her head. It also seems that she was heard screaming there too. Later that same month the *South Wales Echo* contained the following article:

> ' *'Haunted' Collieries. An Explanation.* A colliery expert relates apropos of the sound heard in the Glyncorrwg Level that intermittent gas blowers in collieries are not of uncommon occurrence. When coal gas is forced through a small aperture or fissure it produces a sound closely resembling a scream, and in his experience he has known it to be a very piercing and harrowing scream. On one occasion he went down into his colliery on a Sunday and admits that he would have run away but for the fact that the 'screams' came from behind him. He was obliged to make investigations, and found that a blower has asserted itself which, left to itself, would have filled the workings with gas, and an explosion would probably have occurred when the men returned to work. '

Whether or not the strike at Glyncorrwg avoided some catastrophe isn't known (certainly there was no major accident there) but, obviously, miners' superstitions of this sort did play a very *real* role in saving lives.

In March 1890 a ghostly white bird — again, regarded as being a portent of terrible things to come — was apparently seen perched on top of the winding gear at Morfa colliery at Taibach, near Port Talbot. The following day many of the miners employed there refused to go underground because of the sighting. According to some sources, it was one of a succession of such warnings. In the previous few weeks there had been a strong scent of lilies pervading the mine. Rather more dramatically, hundreds of rats had been seen scurrying from the mine before the start of one of the night shifts, deserting it as they would a sinking ship. Finally, corpse candles (*Canwyll corff*), flickering blue lights said to presage death, were seen in the mine. It was too much for some of the Morfa colliery miners. And it proved just as well that they didn't go down into the mine, decided to heed such 'warnings'; that morning — the 9th March 1890 — there was a huge explosion at Morfa colliery. Eighty seven of their workmates were killed. Their worst fears had been dramatically — and tragically — confirmed.

The Neath correspondent of the *Western Mail* later reported:

'The loss of life is fearful, but it would have been far greater had some of the men not been kept away from work by illness, while others had been led to stay away from work, yielding to strange vague forebodings of coming ill — feelings which some would regard as superstition. It was certain that what had been regarded as omens had been common talk among the men for some weeks past.'

It also seems that some of the Morfa colliery miners regarded the mine as being haunted anyway. Not only had the ghostly sound of roof-falls been heard there, they said, but cries for help had been heard too and strange figures seen in some of the tunnels. Some of them claimed that the figures were the ghosts of some of their former colleagues. Others reported seeing ghostly miners leading phantom pit-ponies and coal-carts through the workings. In the weeks leading up to the disaster all of these were reported too — adding to the miners growing sense of unease about what was about to befall them, about what was about to befall the Morfa colliery.

Just south of Taibach lies Margam. The picturesque remains of the 12th century Cistercian priory here (boasting a famous orangery founded from a cargo of orange trees rescued from a Spanish ship wrecked on the coast during the reign of Queen

Mary) are said to be haunted by the ghost of a monk wearing the Cistercians' customary white habit. The whole site has also been described as possessing an extremely haunted 'atmosphere' — despite the fact that it now finds itself enclosed within the family-fun tourist-trap of Margam Park. A nearby farmhouse, once a grange of the abbey, is also said to be haunted by the phantom monk. Sightings of his ghost have been reported here and so too have the sounds of religious chanting.

Back, now, to Margam Park.

The park is dominated by Margam Castle, a spectacular Tudor/Gothic mansion completed in 1840 for Sir Christopher Rice Mansel Talbot, whose family gave Port Talbot its name. The house is said to have two ghosts: a White Lady and a male figure dressed in Victorian-style clothing. Both ghosts are reputedly most often to be seen at the head of the main staircase in the house.

At Port Talbot itself the ruins of Aberavon Castle were once said to be haunted by a White Lady too. In the 19th century the area was levelled to make way for redevelopment, however, and since then no more sightings of the forlorn-looking figure in the white dress have been reported.

In *Apparitions in Wales*, a book published in 1767, the Rev. Edmund Jones records that a farmhouse in the nearby Ffrwdwyllt valley was once haunted by a ghost which not only slammed doors, blew out candles and snatched at bedclothes, but actually struck people. On one occasion, apparently, it struck the farmer, William Thomas, in the face while he was shaving. On another occasion it hit one of the maids over the head with a cushion as she was walking downstairs. The same maid also had hot water thrown over her on a number of occasions. And it wasn't only members of the household who were subject to such experiences. On at least two occasions the ghost (or possibly poltergeist) turned its attentions on visitors to the house. One of William Thomas' neighbours, staying in the house overnight, was startled out of his evening prayers, when he heard a loud bang in the bedroom he was in. It was like a gunshot, he reported. At the same time something struck the actual bedstead and caused the whole house to shake. Another overnight guest, the Rev. Tibbet, visiting from Montgomeryshire, not only had his bedclothes snatched at, but had his bed moved around the room.

Eventually, it seems that William Thomas decided enough was enough. 'In the name of God' he ordered the spirit to leave the house. Apparently, it did so — but only after it had spoken to William Thomas and had him 'remove certain items' from the house.

At Baglan, just north of Port Talbot, a ghostly figure, thought to be that of a miner killed in an accident at the old Cwmavon ironworks, is said to haunt Mynydd-y-Gaer, the mountain above the town. On its rare and fleeting appearances it is reputed to point to an old airshaft which once serviced the works before then disappearing again.

The same area is also held, in local tradition, to be haunted by Bronwen, whose ghost walks the mountain on certain summer nights. It is here that she was said to meet her lover, Gwilym. The story has it that her brother, Cynfyn, disapproved of her relationship with the latter and tried to end it. One summer night he did so — decisively. He went up onto the mountain and attacked Gwilym while he was waiting there for Bronwen to meet him. The two were soon embroiled in a vicious sword-fight. Cynfyn dealt Gwilym a fatal blow. However, he also received one himself. When Bronwen arrived on the scene it was to find both of them dead, having died of their wounds. Such was her grief at finding both her brother and her lover lying dead on the mountainside that she took Cynfyn's sword and impaled herself upon it.

North, in the Vale of Neath, 'The Devil's Glen', just beyond Crag-y-Dinas, is said to be haunted . . . by a White Lady.

In Neath itself there are several ghost stories.

Neath Abbey (again, founded in the 12th century by the Cistercian order) is said to be haunted by the ghost of the inept and infantile Edward II. The King fled to the abbey when his French wife, Isabella, and his barons sided together and rebelled against him in November 1326. One of the monks — who was later expelled from the order for violating the abbey's strict rules of sanctuary — betrayed him. He was captured near Llantrisant in a valley now known as Pant-y-Brad (The Vale of Treachery). From there he was taken to Berkeley Castle where, after being forced to abdicate, he was murdered. His ghost, it seems, is never actually seen at Neath Abbey — but is said to be heard pounding on the walls.

Victoria Gardens are said to be haunted by one of the famous 'Merched y Mera' (Women of the Mera). These were gypsy women whose children took their maternal rather than their paternal name and who roamed South Wales throughout the 19th century selling various wares from wicker-baskets. It is with her basket that the figure of the woman is supposed to be seen — standing quietly beneath the trees, to then disappear as soon as she is approached.

It was yet another White Lady who was said to haunt Gnoll House. Built in the late 18th century, the house was demolished in 1956, but its grounds still exist — and these are still said to be haunted the ghost, thought to be that of Lady Grant who was widowed while still a young woman shortly after moving into Gnoll House in around 1810. She is said still to be in mourning for her husband.

Finally, it is said that the ghost of a young woman who committed suicide by drowning herself in the River Neath can sometimes be heard sobbing on the riverbank. A methodist schoolteacher from Aberdulais, the story told about her is that she fell in love with a man who often visited Neath while on business. Despite her mother's warnings about him, the lovestruck schoolteacher lavished him with both money and gifts. He, in turn, promised that he would marry her — but only once her mother was dead.

The schoolteacher's mother did eventually die. Her lover then not only failed to keep his promise to her; he never returned to Neath at all. Devastated both by this and by her mother's death, the schoolteacher left a suicide note in a coal-bucket by the side of her fireplace . . . and then made her way down to the river and her tragic end.

Swansea can lay claim to at least three ghost stories.

Built in the mid 1700's by the Dilwyn family who controlled much of the city's china industry, Penllergaer Mansion, which stood on the outskirts of Swansea, was demolished in 1961 after being left empty for over twenty years. At one time, however, it was reputed to be haunted; strange figures were said to drift through its rooms and one of its owners, the well-known South Wales industrialist Sir John Llewellyn, refused to enter the cellar unaccompanied. There were sudden, unexplained 'draughts' in the grounds, stories about the house continue, and watchdogs would crouch and whimper there.

The city's Grand Theatre, meanwhile, is said to be haunted by the colourful Edwardian singer Adelina Patti (born in Madrid, brought up in New York, dazzled 19th century Europe with her singing and sumptuous lifestyle . . . retired to a Gothic Castle, Craig-y-Nos, at the head of the Swansea valley with her Italian lover, the tenor Signor Niccolini, and died there in 1920). Her ghost is said to have been seen in a box at the theatre on several occasions over the years. In *Portrait of Gower* (1976) Wynford Vaughan Thomas wrote:

'I was recently talking to a well-known TV producer who had once played Swansea in her early repertory days. She told me a curious story. She was rehearsing one morning on the empty stage when she looked up at one of the boxes. She saw a beautiful lady in rich Edwardian costume lean forward and give polite applause to the act. She turned to a stage hand to ask who was in the box but when she looked again the lady had vanished. Said the stage hand, 'We all know her — it's Madame Patti.' Indeed the great Adelina Patti used to occupy this box when she came down to Swansea to grace charity concerts with her presence.'

A lady of somewhat less esteemed profession is said to haunt the Ford Motor Company works at Swansea; it is thought that she once worked as prostitute, picking up sailors at Jersey Marine. Known as 'Jersey Lil', some stories about her have it that she was murdered by one of her clients, others that she met her death in even less salubrious circumstances; by falling into a pickling vat at the Elba pickling works (where she may have worked during the day). Either way, before her emergence at the Ford factory — where, reportedly, she has been seen on a number of occasions — she was also said to haunt the Elba tin-plate works at Jersey Marine.

Beyond Swansea lies the beautiful peninsula of the Gower — grassy cliffs and sandy, unspoilt beaches to the south; vast estuarine marshes to the north. Stories of smuggling and shipwrecks abound here . . . and so, too, do ghost stories.

Oystermouth Castle at Mumbles dates from the 13th century. Here there is said to be a White Lady who sometimes appears outside the castle walls. She is usually said to be seen sobbing and to have the top half of her dress torn away to reveal her back — which is covered in blood. The story goes that she is the ghost of a woman who was whipped to death at the whipping-post (which can still be seen) in the castle's dungeon. Why she should have been so brutally put to death isn't known.

Legend has it that where the lighthouse now stands at Mumbles Head there was once a small cell, located in a cave in the rocks, which was occupied by an elderly monk. One evening, shortly after sunset, the story continues, the monk saw a boat being rowed towards him. The men in the boat then brought the body of a well dressed young man ashore. They had, it seemed, murdered him. The men asked the monk to say some prayers for the repose of their victim's soul. The monk agreed. The men then laid the young man's body in the cave, left some money for the monk (in all probability having stolen it from the murdered young man to begin with) — and rowed away again. The story concludes that, despite the monk's efforts, the murdered man's spirit still cries out from the cave to be given burial in consecrated ground. His soul, it seems, didn't find repose after all.

In Titchbourne Street, Mumbles, there is a house owned by hospital Chaplain, the Rev. Borthwick, which was once a blacksmith's forge. Some three hundred years old and with some of its walls over a yard thick, the house now appears to be haunted by the blacksmith. Neither the Rev. Borthwick nor any of his family have seen the ghost, but he describes the 'presence' as somehow having a masculine feeling to it. The ghost isn't unfriendly, he adds, but mischievous.

Having bought the house in the mid 80's, the Rev. Borthwick, first had its ghostly inhabitant brought to his attention by some of his neighbours who were surprised that the previous owner hadn't informed him of some of the strange occurrences which had taken place there. But in any event he soon discovered these for himself. Windows were regularly flung open throughout the house, even in winter. When he and his wife went to a DIY store in Swansea to buy a timer to control the heating in the house they were then astonished to witness an even more bizarre phenomenon. The various products hanging on the hooks where they were selecting the timer suddenly started to cascade onto the floor, bringing one of the store's attendants rushing to see what all the commotion was. Lights were turned on and off in the house. When Mrs Borthwick placed a flower vase on a linen cloth she returned some moments later to discover the vase turned upside down, the cloth pushed inside it. The Borthwick's daughter, a student at the University of Swansea, heard footsteps in the house. A friend of hers, staying in the house overnight, dreamt that she was having cold water poured over her. She awoke to discover that — inexplicably — water had indeed soaked the bed. On another occasion some of her friends came to the house to watch a rugby match on television. Jokingly, someone suggested that she should have the ghost turn it on for them. It did so. Since then, says the Rev. Borthwick, their mischievous ghost has rarely failed to provide such demonstrations of its presence when requested to do so; turning lights on and off or opening windows as though performing party-tricks. It is, he concludes, a ghost with which he feels quite at ease, which he sees no need to exorcise.

Onto the Gower peninsula proper.

Pennard Castle, like Oystermouth Castle, is Norman in origin. It is, however, much less well preserved. In fact, it was abandoned shortly after it was built because of the encroachment of drifting sand which rendered it quite uninhabitable. (On the other hand, for the record, there is also a folk-tale which relates how a band of fairies caused a sandstorm to overwhelm the castle after the Norman lord there attacked them one night while they were dancing outside the castle walls.) Here there is said to be yet another Gwrach y Rhibyn — this guarding a hidden treasure buried somewhere in the sand-dunes near the castle ruins. Legend warns that anyone who sleeps within the castle walls risks being cursed by her. And so, legend continues, a young man who once slept there for a bet discovered. The following morning he was found lying unconscious on one of the dunes, his body badly bruised, his face scored with several deep scratches. From that moment on he was deranged; never recovering from whatever ordeal it was that he had been through during the night. Of course locals were sure that they knew what had happened to him: he had been attacked by the Gwrach y Rhibyn.

Oxwich Bay, one of the most well-known beaches on the Gower, also has a curious folk-tale told about it; this telling of a ceffyl-dŵr (water-horse) which was once seen — walking slowly along on its hind legs — on the narrow path leading to St Illtud's church which overlooks the bay.

Rather more traditionally, the bay is also said to be haunted by the ghostly sounds of two of Gower's warring smuggling families — the Mansells and their rivals the Herberts — fighting over their spoils on the beach. The same phenomenon is also said to be heard at Rhossili Bay further to the west, where the two families would also frequently unload their smuggled gains.

At Port Eynon Bay, only a short distance west of Oxwich, stood the Salt House. This was built during the reign of Henry VIII by David Lucas for his son, John.

John Lucas was, by all accounts, a man of 'fierce and ungovernable violence'. He turned Salt House into a stronghold from which to conduct his considerable smuggling activities. In league with the younger members of the Mansell family from nearby Henllys, he then embarked on a lifetime career of piracy. His activities soon infuriated the authorities, in London as well as Swansea, but locals remained firmly on his side; it being his wont — like some sort of Robin Hood figure — to divide some of the profits from his 'business' between them.

When John Lucas died, his sons took over where he had left off. The Lucases continued in their 'family business' for generations. The deep cellars beneath the Salt House were kept full of illicit liquor and other smuggled goods for years; throughout the whole of the 17th century. But then, in 1703, the Gower — in common with the rest of Britain — was lashed by exceptionally violent storms. The notorious bolt-hole of the Salt House was flooded. Part of the building collapsed when it was struck by lightning. It was abandoned, left a ruin.

In the 19th century some cottages were built on the site of the old Salt House. It is the ruins of these which still stand at Port Eynon Point.

They are, almost inevitably, said to be haunted by the ghosts of the smugglers who once made such a name for themselves there.

Between Port Eynon and Rhossili — along one of the many beautiful coastal paths to be found on Gower — is Paviland Cave. In 1823 the Rev. William Buckland, the first Professor of Geology at Oxford University (and a future Dean of Westminster), unearthed a headless human skeleton in the cave, the bones of which were stained brick-red. His discovery, one of the most sensational archaeological finds of the time, was duly christened the Red Lady; the Rev. Buckland having decided that the remains were those of a woman who had been buried in the cave in Roman-Britain times. Ghost stories began to develop around the discovery: that the Red Lady — a hideous, witch-like old crone — now haunted the cave, her ghost clambering around inside its dark depths, screaming curses from ledges and from behind fallen rocks. In 1923 the cave was re-excavated and it was determined that the human remains which the Rev. Buckland had discovered were, in fact, those of a male youth of the Cro-Magnon race (an early form of modern *homo sapiens*). The bones, it seemed, had been stained with red ochre — possibly as part of some sort of burial ceremony. Despite these revelations, stories of the Red Lady haunting Paviland Cave persisted undiminished.

On the magnificent stretch of beach of Rhosili Bay — sweeping from Worms Head to Burry Holms, overlooked by the lush Rhossili Downs and washed by long Atlantic rollers (and with the wooden ribs of the 1887 wreck of the Helvetia still protruding from the sands below Rhossili itself) — a phantom coach is said to appear on stormy nights, drawn by four grey horses and driven by a member of the (in)famous Mansell family. The story behind the haunting has it that one stormy night sometime during the 17th century a Spanish bullion ship was washed up on the beach. Before the lord of the manor could lay claim to it, however, the member of the Mansell family in question drove a coach out to the wreck and plundered it for himself; carrying away a fortune in silver. Tradition has it though that his spoils brought him nothing but ill-luck — and the story ends that he was murdered shortly afterwards. (For those inclined to test their own luck, as it were, coins and other items from wrecked ships are still occasionally found in Rhossili Bay — usually after the sand has been stirred up following winter storms.)

Two hundred feet down from Rhossili village on the clifftop and at the foot of the Rhossili Downs where they reach the beach, lie the sand-dunes known as the Warren. A 'lost' village, including its church, is buried here. It is thought that it was overwhelmed by the sands — and, accordingly, abandoned — sometime during the 13th century. Human remains have been discovered here and the site is said to be haunted.

Overlooking the bay — set in splendid isolation above the beach on the lower slopes of the Rhossili Downs — stands the Old Rectory. Its unusual situation is explained by the fact that the incumbent vicar once had to serve both Rhossili and the neighbouring village of Llangennith to the north: the rectory was simply built between the two. It was only much later that the church authorities decided to built a new rectory close to Rhossili church and so end the vicars' 'exile'. The Old Rectory is said to be haunted, as Wynford Vaughan Thomas recorded in *Portrait of Gower* (1976):

> 'One person who stayed in the house, after the Church authorities had wisely built a new Rectory near to Rhossili Church, told me that on certain winter's nights 'something very unpleasant indeed comes out of the sea and comes into the house'. Another story suggests that you can suddenly walk into a cold pool of air in the corridor and hear a low voice in your ear saying, 'Why don't you turn around and look at me?' No one has ever dared.'

Further north, the remote, low-lying spur of Whitford Point is now owned by the National Trust (as is much of the area around Rhossili, of course). It combines impressive sand-dunes with expansive pine-plantations. At the furthest end of the point stands an elegant forty-four foot cast-iron tower built in 1854. This housed a light which guided ships leaving Burry Port out into Camarthen Bay. It is still used today.

In January 1868 — on a still night and with the sea calm — some eighteen 80-400 tons sailing ships, laden with coal, were towed out of Llanelli by tugs. They cast off and rounded Whitford Point intending to clear Burry Holms on the ebb tide. No sooner had he passed the point, however, than the wind suddenly died on them. The tide then turned and the ships found themselves caught on a heavy swell which began to run through the channel. They dropped anchor, but to no avail; their anchors were torn loose. Disaster soon overtook the stricken ships. Some were thrown about so violently that their hulls were split wide open. Others were dashed onto the rocks at Broughton Bay or collided with one another. Within the space of an hour sixteen of the ships had been wrecked. Back on shore no one was aware of what happened.

The following morning the entire coast from Whitford Sker to Burry Holms was littered with shattered timbers, coal and corpses. The dead were duly buried at Llanmadoc and Llangennith. Again, in *Portrait of Gower* (1976), Wynford Vaughan Thomas refers to the incident, recording a story told by the Rev. J. D. Davies, rector of Cheriton and Llanmadoc, who wrote several books about the Gower peninsula between 1877 and 1898:

> 'The choir of the Parish happened on the evening in question, to be holding their weekly practice in the church, when suddenly an indescribable scream of terror was heard in the churchyard, as of one in the last extremity of mortal fear. I immediately ran out to see what was the matter, and saw a young lad, whom I knew quite well, standing in the middle of the walk, not far from the porch, with his face not only blanched, but actually distorted with fright. 'What is the matter, my lad?' I asked. 'Oh,' he replied, 'I saw a man without his hat come and look in at the window.' I brought the poor terrified lad into the church, where he remained some little time before he came to himself. It was currently believed that what he saw was the apparition of one of the poor seamen who was drowned, as it was just about the time when the wreck took place.'

Moving east again, the ancient Welcome to Town inn in the village of Llanrhidian is said to be haunted by the ghost of a coachman dressed in Regency-style clothes. He has, reportedly, been seen sitting in the bar there on a number of occasions.

East of Llanrhidian lies Llanellan. Little remains of this 'lost' village now: a few scattered stones, the grass covered outlines of various foundations. The story here is that the survivors of a long-ago shipwreck — their ship grounded in the estuary — were given shelter in the village. Within days, however, it became all too apparent that the survivors of the wreck wouldn't survive for long; they were all afflicted with plague. Of course, it was only a short matter of time before the villagers succumbed too. No one survived. The entire village was wiped out. A White Lady is now said to haunt the site of the village — and it is thought to be unlucky to touch any of the old stones there.

Selected Bibliography

Chris Barber, *Ghosts of Wales*, John Jones, 1979

Alison Bielski, *The Story of St Mellons*, Alun Books, 1985

Stanley W. Bevan, *St Brides Major, Southerndown & Ogmore-by-Sea*, D Browne & Sons Ltd., 1980

J. A. Brooks, *Ghosts and Legends of Wales*, Jarrold, 1987

R. L. Brown, *Turn of the Century Tongwynlais*, Roger Brown, 1982

Stephen Clarke, *The Most Haunted House in Monmouth*, Monmouth Archaeological Society, 1975

Stephen Clarke, *Ghosts and Legends of Monmouth and Hereford*, Monmouth Archaeological Society, 1975

Jeanette Dixon, *Welsh Ghosts*, James Pike Ltd., 1975

Alun Evans & William Willis, *Ghosts and Legends of the Vale of Neath*, Glamorgan Press, 1987

Lord Halifax, *Lord Halifax's Ghost Book*, Didier, 1937

S. C. & A. M. Hall, *The Book of South Wales, the Wye and the Coast*, Arthur Hall, Virtue & Co., 1861

Fred J. Hando, *Out and About in Monmouthshire*, R. H. Johns, 1958

Glyn M. Jones & Elfyn Scourfield, *Sully*, South Western Printers, 1986

Thomas Lloyd, *The Lost Houses of Wales*, Save Britain's Heritage, 1986

Roberta Ross Powell, *Welsh Tales of the Supernatural*, John Jones, 1979

Jane Pugh, *Welsh Ghosts and Phantoms*, Celtic Educational Services, 1979

Jane Pugh, *Welsh Ghostly Encounters*, Gwasg Carreg Gwalch, 1990

Alan Roderick, *Folklore of Glamorgan*, Village Publishing, 1986

Margaret R. Shanahan, *Ghosts of Glamorgan*, Transactions of the Port Talbot Historical Society, 1963

Wirt Sikes, *Rambles in Old South Wales*, Stewart Williams, 1881

Wynford Vaughan Thomas, *Portrait of Gower*, Hale, 1976

Marie Trevelyan, *Folklore and Folk Stories of Wales*, Eliot Stock, 1909

Peter Underwood, *Ghosts of Wales*, Christopher Davies, 1978

Barry & District News

Cardiff Independent

Cardiff Leader

Cardiff News

Cardiff & Suburban News

South Wales Echo

Western Mail